T3-BSF-125

Assessment for the New Curriculum: A Guide for Professional Accounting Programs

Joanne Gainen, Ph.D.
Paul Locatelli, S.J.
Santa Clara University

Copyright, Accounting Education Change Commission and
American Accounting Association, 1995
All rights reserved.
ISBN 0-86539-079-7
Printed in the United States of America

American Accounting Association
5717 Bessie Drive
Sarasota, Florida 34233

657.07
G142as

CONTENTS

ACKNOWLEDGEMENTS

We are indebted to the AECC Task Force on Assessment (Dave Landsittel [Chair], Bob Elliott, Penny Flugger, Barron Harvey, Bill Shenkir, and Jean Wyer) for the insights they offered as we articulated our view of the "culture of evidence" applied to accounting education. We are especially grateful to Dave Landsittel, Bob Elliott, and Jean Wyer for their close readings of early drafts. Rich Flaherty of the AECC patiently yet with astonishing speed managed the prepublication process, and with Jan Williams arranged joint publication with the AAA and AECC.

We gratefully acknowledge Peter Ewell of the National Center for Higher Education Management Systems for his thoughtful advice and the research materials he shared with us. We had help along the way from Freida Bayer (University of Texas), Patrick McKenzie (Arizona State University), Irvin Tom Nelson (Utah State University), Susan Perry (University of Virginia), Jay Smith (Brigham Young University), and the faculty of the Accounting Department at Santa Clara University. They encouraged us to develop a *practical* model and contributed materials to illustrate assessment practice in accounting education today.

Thanks also to Heather Rush of Word and Image, who designed our graphics and diplomatically but firmly trimmed our prose. Finally, we are grateful for the daily assistance of George Giacomini, Joan Murphy, Marlene Robles-Cheney, and Nora Jamison, all of Santa Clara University. Each contributed tremendous support to the completion of this project.

FOREWORD

Since its formation in 1989, the Accounting Education Change Commission has devoted its efforts to the mission of improving the academic preparation of accountants, so that entrants to the profession would possess the skills, knowledge, and values and attitudes required for success in accounting career paths. This mission is consistent with the objectives of the American Accounting Association's Bedford Committee Report and the Sponsoring Firms' white paper, *"Perspectives on Education: Capabilities for Success in the Accounting Profession."*

The Commission adopted three major thrusts—faculty development, curriculum development and dissemination, and assessment. Assessment initiatives included a requirement that each of the AECC grant schools develop an assessment plan and workshops on assessment for the grant schools and other schools. Also, the Commission supported the preparation and publication of this monograph to help accounting educators develop practical and effective assessment programs. The monograph provides background on the assessment movement in the U.S., outlines a model for developing an assessment program, provides guidance for faculty to assess not only the traditional learning outcomes but also the expanded learning outcomes advocated by the AECC and others, and illustrates the use of assessment as a tool for continuous improvement of learning outcomes and client satisfaction. Many examples are provided from current assessment practices.

As the authors indicate, the value of assessment is to provide a "culture of evidence" and an inquiring spirit that leads to questions that translate into action to improve learning outcomes. Administrative and faculty support is necessary for the culture of evidence to become the standard of practice in accounting education.

The authors of this guide bring complementary perspectives to the challenge of assessment in accounting education. Dr. Joanne Gainen is director of the Teaching and Learning Center at Santa Clara University, where she has coordinated numerous assessment projects. She also conducts training and has published on critical thinking, intellectual development, classroom research, and new faculty mentoring. Rev. Paul Locatelli, S.J., is President of Santa Clara University and has been a member of the Accounting Education Change Commission since its founding in 1989. He has served on numerous accreditation boards and in 1994 was named Outstanding Accounting Educator of the Year by the California Society of CPAs. The Commission is very grateful to the authors for their efforts in preparing this guide.

Richard E. Flaherty
Executive Director
Accounting Education Change Commission
Tempe, Arizona
December 1994

Introduction
THE PROMISE OF ASSESSMENT: RESOURCE FOR CHANGE IN ACCOUNTING EDUCATION

One of the objectives of the Accounting Education Change Commission (AECC) is to increase the effectiveness of academic programs in preparing students to enter a "dynamic, complex, expanding and constantly changing profession" (AECC, *Objectives*, 1990, p. 1). The AECC further notes that accounting graduates must function in a global economy which is increasingly sophisticated and interdependent. The current effort to change accounting education is directed toward the achievement of this AECC objective.

The AECC and the accounting community in general call for a change of focus in the philosophy of accounting education. Currently, accounting programs are aimed at transmitting technical knowledge, while the new focus envisions helping students to develop a deep understanding of concepts and policies, as well as developing skills and attitudes necessary for the successful practice of accounting. This transformation is intended to produce graduates better prepared to function within the profession by:

- Developing the knowledge, skills, and values of the discipline
- Knowing and conforming to the ethics of the profession
- Being able to make better value judgments
- Maintaining a high level of integrity, objectivity, competence, and concern for public interest (*Objectives*, pp. 2-3)

The six major accounting firms have invested $5 million since 1989 to help advance the AECC's vision. This investment has taken the form of direct grants to accounting programs, participation in accounting publication efforts, and funding of general information programs to disseminate the changing concept of accounting education. It soon became clear that few schools or accounting programs had suitable metrics in place to measure the success of their efforts in achieving these new learning objectives. In particular, the new emphasis on lifelong learning challenged accounting educators to create new assessment methods and measures.

After visiting schools that have recently revised their curricula, one observer noted that "Dedicated academics are striving to design outstanding learning environments. Visitors can only wonder at the diversity of solutions."

This diversity raises the questions, "Is one [solution] 'better than others? Will the outcomes differ? Will the accounting environment in the 21st Century resemble any of these solutions?"

Continuous improvement requires continuous evaluation based on credible evidence systematically obtained. Recognizing this, the AECC:

- Encouraged grant recipients to develop and implement assessment plans
- Sponsored workshops on assessment for grant institutions
- Commissioned this guide to increase the use of assessment in program improvement

---

Educational Assessment
is the systematic collection, interpretation, and use of information about
Student Characteristics,
Educational Environment,
Learning Outcomes
and Client Satisfaction
to improve student performance and professional success.

0.1 Purposes of this Guide

This guide was commissioned by the AECC to help accounting educators develop practical, effective assessment programs to provide information for curricular and instructional improvement. "Improvement" in this context is broadly defined to reflect the diverse educational environments, curricular goals, approaches to curricular change, and organizational cultures of accounting programs nationally.

The guide responds to recurring faculty questions and concerns about assessment. It has four objectives:

- To inform accounting educators about the imperatives driving the assessment movement
- To provide practical guidance for faculty in the development of methods to assess expanded learning outcomes (often referred to as outcomes) such as those advocated by the AECC, professional accounting associations, and the AACSB
- To identify student characteristics and factors in the educational environment that influence those outcomes
- To illustrate the use of assessment as a tool for continuous improvement of learning outcomes and client satisfaction

The guide outlines a model for developing the department's assessment program. It suggests ways to establish assessment priorities, and outlines methods for clarifying curricular goals to facilitate curriculum development and assessment. It provides suggestions for framing questions about the curriculum and assessment, measuring improvement, and using what is learned to improve program outcomes and client satisfaction. Throughout the guide, readers will find examples from current assessment practices at AECC grant-funded schools and other institutions in the forefront of curricular change and assessment in accounting education.

0.2 Structure of the Guide

The remainder of the guide is in two parts.

Part I *outlines* the planning framework.
Chapter 1 puts assessment into a larger educational context.
Chapter 2 identifies key stakeholders and participants in the process.
Chapter 3 previews the model for accounting education assessment planning.

Part II *elaborates* on this framework.
Chapter 4 discusses the process of establishing purposes and priorities for the assessment program.
Chapter 5 identifies budgeting and resource allocation issues.
Chapter 6 describes the essential process of articulating program goals, as well as clarifying the distinction between *goals* and *objectives or performance outcomes*.
Chapter 7 explains how to translate goals into measurable objectives.
Chapter 8 identifies research design topics and suggests ways to initiate an assessment program.
Chapter 9 describes the development of learning outcome measurement. It is structured to mirror the three major categories of learning outcomes endorsed by the AECC:

- Expanded professional knowledge
- Improved skills (intellectual, interpersonal, communication, and ethical reasoning)
- Enhanced professional orientation (values and attitudes essential for professional integrity and lifelong learning)

This chapter provides guidance in designing more reliable performance measures. It also suggests practical methods for data collection.
Chapter 10 presents strategies to assess contributions of the educational environment.
Chapter 11 discusses reporting and use of assessment results.
Chapter 12 advocates review and improvement of the assessment process itself.
The guide concludes with a *Glossary* and *Bibliography* of assessment resources.

Throughout the text, *Figures* summarize key points and present tools from the literature on assessment. *Tables* at the end of each chapter illustrate application of concepts presented in that chapter. *Appendices* present materials drawn from current assessment practice in accounting.

Designing an assessment program is an iterative process. Each new phase leads to insights that stimulate rethinking of earlier phases. Assessment facilitates improvement by sharpening curricular focus and academic effectiveness. It also establishes a sense of common purpose among faculty members as they come to appreciate their individual and collective contributions to the success of their programs' graduates.

0.3 Definition of Assessment

Assessment is the systematic collection, interpretation, and use of information on student characteristics, the educational environment, and learning outcomes to improve student learning and satisfaction.

This document emphasizes the comparison of *expected* with *actual* student learning outcomes, and the continuous use of process and outcome information, to identify strengths and weaknesses in students' performance and influences on the outcomes observed.

"Expected outcomes" are often stated as "performance criteria" (Chapter 9). In statistical analyses, they take into account entering student characteristics. "Actual outcomes" take into account both student characteristics and features of the educational environment to which individual students are exposed.

The assessment framework is shown below:

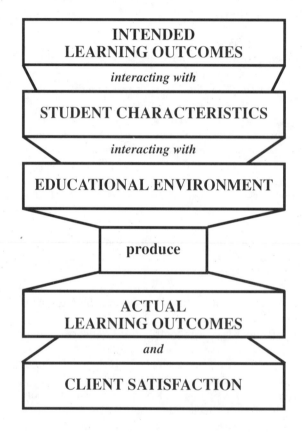

The mission and goals of the program, institution, and profession influence these elements (Baker and others, 1993; Gardiner, 1989). Learning outcomes, in particular, reflect these objectives, and those of the faculty and students.

Faculty regularly assess the performance of *individual* students, but assessment involves compiling evidence about individual students' performance from multiple perspectives to understand learning at the *program* level. In program-level assessment, faculty and other stakeholders clarify learning goals and set performance parameters. These criteria serve as internal benchmarks against which students' performance can be measured. Evidence from multiple sources is integrated over time to understand relationships among learning outcomes, student characteristics, and contributions of the educational environment. Information from these sources guides revision of current programs or development of new initiatives aimed at improving student learning.

0.4 *Assessment:* Timely, Practical Information for Educational Decision Making

Assessment adds the greatest value to educational programs when it provides current information that can be *quickly* integrated into the ongoing process of instruction and curriculum revision. Assessment should enable faculty to monitor students' performance and client satisfaction *continuously* so that program effectiveness can be enhanced. Delaying assessment until the end of a curricular "experiment" (particularly if the end is defined as the point when the first class of students graduates from a new or revised program) eliminates opportunities to improve the curriculum for students within *that* program. From this perspective, assessment becomes an *information function for educational decision-making*, much as accounting is now understood as an *information function for financial decision-making* (Bedford Report, 1986; Diamond and Pincus, 1994; Elliott, 1991). Assessment, therefore, encourages educators to generate new information about what and how students are learning in the current program, and what and how they should be learning from the program in the future.

Unlike traditional laboratory research, assessment is problem-oriented and field-based. Its primary purpose is to help educators improve program processes and outcomes, rather than to test theoretical knowledge. It therefore works on different principles of design than those associated with laboratory research. Realistically, formal experiments involving random assignment to experimental and control groups are seldom possible. Still, it *is* possible to obtain valid, useful information working within the constraints of the educational environment. This guide suggests practical ways to acquire and use such information for thoughtful and continuous program improvement.

Although this guide describes a comprehensive model for planning assessment, implementation is inevitably incremental. Once the key players and stakeholders have been identified (Chapter 2), and the basic framework for assessment is clearly understood (Chapter 3), the assessment committee should clarify the purposes and scope of the assessment (Chapters 4 and 5), and goals of the curriculum (Chapter 6) before discussing specific measures. Program documents should be consulted to identify priorities for assessment.

Once the faculty have identified essential goals, the department should decide on a strategy for organizing the assessment. Options include:

- Focusing assessment on a particular area of the curriculum, such as communication skills or proficiency in using technological information
- Pilot testing a particular approach to assessment, for example, compiling portfolios of students' work, or establishing a database to track students' progress and identify contributing factors
- Targeting a specific student population to study closely

In any case, the assessment program should be consistent with the interests, culture, and resources of the department and school.

In the long run, the value of assessment is not to provide *numerical* indicators of success or failure, nor to design the definitive curricular experiment. Its value is to create a "culture of evidence" (Wolff, 1990) that prompts the institution to ask questions — questions that lead to the development of information to improve the learning outcomes for all entering students. The goal is to develop an inquiring spirit into questions about the program that translate into action research projects and ongoing commitment to self-scrutiny.

In this culture, assessment is a tool that will help accounting educators create educational environments for the 21st century, based on evidence of what works for the students they are responsible to educate.

ASSESSMENT PROCESS

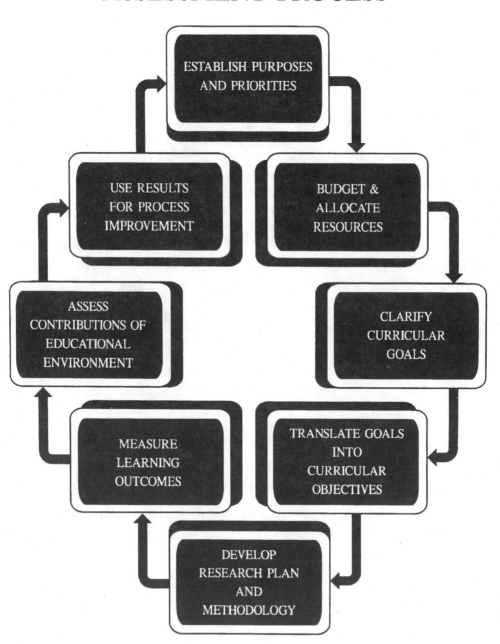

PART I UNDERSTANDING ASSESSMENT

Chapter 1
THE CONTEXT FOR ASSESSMENT

This chapter examines:

- The significance of assessment
- The external rationale for assessment
- Internal perspectives on assessment, including faculty concerns
- Standards and principles of good practice for assessment

1.1. Significance of the Assessment Movement

The assessment movement is part of a paradigm shift in discussions of educational quality. These discussions increasingly focus on the achievement of *expanded* learning outcomes — knowledge, skills, and professional values and attitudes — and an understanding of how those outcomes are achieved.

First, assessment has broadened the scope for determining educational quality. Traditionally, institutional quality has been determined primarily on the basis of resources, reputation, and selectivity in admissions. Assessment today seeks evidence that the intended learning outcomes of higher education have been achieved. The philosophy behind this movement is that educational institutions should be in the business of increasing access to education and "developing talent," rather than screening out students who do not fit a narrow set of entrance criteria (Astin, 1985). Much of what students gain from their undergraduate experience is a function of what they bring to it. Today, a comprehensive assessment program *combines* students' characteristics with the educational environment in a multifaceted analysis to understand and improve learning outcomes for *all* students.

Second, in accounting the focus on outcomes has expanded the definition of *learning* beyond traditional interpretations. Expectations of accounting graduates now include indications of professional competence and skills of lifelong learning (AAA Committee on the Future, 1986; AECC *Objectives*, 1990; Deppe, Sonderegger, Stice, Clark, and Streuling, 1991). In addition, professional values and attitudes are now considered important. The AECC *Objectives* emphasize the motivation to continue learning throughout one's career, and the internalization of ethical standards and values of the profession. Expanded curricula found at Brigham Young University (BYU), University of Southern California (USC), Arizona State University (ASU), and others now emphasize information management, complex problem solving, decision making, critical thinking, communication of information, and teamwork, all skills that will encourage students and graduates to continue to learn throughout their lives.

Complex skills and professional orientation have generally been *implicit* in the curriculum. Their emergence as an *explicit* focus of instruction presents new challenges for curriculum development, instruction, and assessment.

Finally, assessment includes strategies to understand the educational environment and its influence on the outcomes observed. This environment includes program content and pedagogy, student-faculty contacts, academic support programs, and co-curricular involvement (such as internships and professional practice projects).

Data on student characteristics, the educational environment, and learning outcomes can be integrated through sophisticated analytical techniques such as multivariate analysis or, when such sophistication is not available, through the discussion of data from a variety of sources.

Because assessment of learning outcomes at the program level is relatively new to higher education, analytical methods and theories are still being developed and tested. For example, performance-based measurement techniques raise new questions of reliability and validity. Current trends also require development of new, more practical methods to obtain evidence about complex abilities and attitudes as well as strategies to integrate assessment information into the total quality improvement efforts of faculty at the classroom and program level.

1.2. The Case for Assessment: Public Policy and Professional Perspectives

The assessment movement in higher education can be traced to a combination of public policy mandates and institutional experiments in the late 1970s (Ewell, 1991b). As an instrument for public policy, assessment can serve the ever-increasing demand for accountability. State legislatures and accrediting agencies now routinely include assessment as a means to validate learning outcomes.

1.2.1 State Mandates and Assessment

Some form of assessment is now mandated in over 40 states, and over 90% of institutions of higher education now claim to have assessment programs (El-Khawas, 1990). What began in the 1980's as experiments by a few institutions (for example, Alverno College, Northeast Missouri State University, King's College, James Madison University, and University of Tennessee) and states (for example, Virginia, New Jersey, and Tennessee) has grown to a formal institutional requirement encouraged or mandated by state governments.

In general, state mandates have left the design of assessment programs to individual institutions to reflect their particular mission and student characteristics. Their intent was to prompt educational institutions to inform the public about program results. More recently, perhaps because some institutions were less than enthusiastic in their compliance, public officials in some states (for example, Missouri, South Carolina, Tennessee) have looked to common, state-wide assessment tools. The rhetoric of accountability has shifted also, from a focus on informing the public to "documenting a concrete return on investment" (Ewell, 1991a, p. 14).

1.2.2 Accreditation and Assessment

Accreditation, whether regional or national, is the process by which judgments of quality are made based on established and approved standards. Most accrediting standards now require some form of assessment based on the individual institution's mission. Accreditation bodies generally do not mandate what form assessment should take; rather, they seek evidence that results exist and are being used for program improvement.

Assessment as evaluation has long been an implicit and explicit part of accreditation, program review, and planning. It has always aimed at ensuring quality and gauging improvement over time; however, a focus on learning outcomes as part of the review process is fairly recent. The current AACSB accreditation standards state that "Each degree program should be systematically monitored to assess its effectiveness." [C.2.2] Monitoring includes evaluation of faculty in their roles as teachers as well as scholars, with attention "to course development, effective teaching, and instructional innovations." [FD.3.b]

AACSB standards for accrediting programs of accounting call for a broad-based assessment process:

> Key factors in the assessment of quality are the qualifications, development, and involvement of faculty; the design and effectiveness of the curriculum; the nature and effectiveness of the instructional processes utilized; the learning resources available to both faculty and students;...[and] the processes in place to plan, assess, and assure quality ... (Preamble).

The standards also emphasize that "The evaluation of the accounting faculty will rely heavily on assessments of teaching effectiveness..." [A-IN.2]. Teaching effectiveness, however, extends beyond the "relevance of course content or suitable instructional methods" to what students take from the course in the form of knowledge, skills, and professional orientation.

The standards correctly suggest an integral relationship between assessment and curricular or instructional change, but observers note that unfortunately the two processes are often perceived as unrelated. The disjunction is evident when institutional self-studies report assessment results in a separate section without linking them to changes implemented or planned (Ewell, 1992, p.14). Without this linkage, assessment becomes an administrative burden rather than a tool for continuous program improvement.

1.2.3 Program Review and Assessment

Program review involves a comprehensive evaluation of such factors as:

- The components and structure of the program
- The qualifications of faculty and students
- The role of research
- The level of financial and information/technology resources available to support the program

Assessment of learning outcomes is increasingly recognized as an important part of program review expected by many state boards and accreditation agencies. In its resource guide for program review, the Association of American Colleges observes that

> the goal of program review should be to increase the self-consciousness of faculty members and administrators about their educational practices so they can improve the quality of teaching and learning (AAC, 1992, p. 1).

Assessment fosters such self-consciousness. In turn, an emphasis on learning in program review suggests opportunities to incorporate outcomes assessment:

> Corporate attention to the ways in which a major works as a total program, rather than as a set of discrete (and often disparate) courses, can establish a series of points at which faculty members both assess and support students' continuing progress in the field (AAC, 1992, p. 27).

Program review is thus broader then assessment. In the current era of accountability, a well designed program review will include assessment of entering student characteristics, the educational environment, and learning outcomes, as well as client satisfaction.

1.2.4 Expectations of the Profession

In a professional field such as accounting, employers, too, have a stake in the results of assessment programs. Employers want evidence that institutions prepare graduates "to *become* professional accountants, not to *be* professional accountants at the time of entry into the profession... and to lay the base on which lifelong learning can be built" (*Objectives*, p. 1). As noted in the Introduction, concerns of leaders in the profession prompted the formation of the AECC to implement changes that would benefit the profession. Assessment benefits the program and its graduates when evidence confirms competencies endorsed by the profession.

An assessment program may also benefit the profession by helping faculty address minority student enrollment and retention. The pool of minority graduates in accounting remains small in relation to the population as a whole, limiting firms' ability to diversify their staff. Minority students, particularly African Americans, express interest in accounting (Carpenter, Friar, and Lipe, 1993), but the programs may not be structured to heighten their interest and progress in the profession. In elementary accounting courses, minority students withdraw at a higher rate than white students. Those that persevere tend to receive lower-than-average grades (Carpenter and others, 1993). Studies to investigate and remedy causes of this phenomenon will help the program attract and retain a more diverse student population. They will also benefit the profession by providing a more diversified and better qualified pool of future employees.

1.3 The Quest for Excellence: Faculty Perspectives on Assessment

The decision to implement a formal assessment program is a choice for quality and continuous improvement that extends beyond individual faculty. Although external mandates provide the catalyst, it is faculty and administrative initiative and commitment to educational quality that will render assessment a meaningful aspect of program development.

1.3.1 Continuous Program Improvement

Continuous quality improvement (originally a goal of businesses operating in a competitive environment) has also become a theme in discussions of the future of higher education (for example, see *Change* [May/June 1993]; *Educational Record* [June, 1993], *NACUBO Business Officer* [December 1993] and numerous issues of the AAHE *Bulletin*). In the business community, quality is generally measured in terms of "bottom-line" results and client satisfaction. In the higher education context, results include both students' performance and the satisfaction of those whom the program serves, most notably students, alumni, and employers.

Assessment for improvement at the classroom and program levels has become more common in recent years. Many faculty use informal classroom evaluation to monitor students' progress and responses during instruction (Angelo, 1991; Angelo and Cross, 1993). Some departments use data available from their university's institutional research office to monitor trends in enrollment, student characteristics, and student or alumni satisfaction. Information to be used to help understand program outcomes can often be obtained from existing senior exit interviews or surveys, scores on standardized tests such as the CPA exam and GMAT, and current student, alumni, and employer surveys.

In addition to these traditional tools, new types of information are needed to evaluate expanded professionally-relevant outcomes. Obtaining and using such information is a major focus of this guide. Faculty review of this information will suggest curricular and instructional changes for continuous improvement of learning outcomes.

1.3.2 Contributions of Assessment to Lifelong Learning

The expanded educational outcomes sought by the profession include an emphasis on *learning-to-learn* skills. Assessment helps faculty advance the development of these skills by:

*   Articulating these goals and relevant performance criteria
*   Encouraging faculty to include learning to learn as part of instruction and assessment in their courses
*   Providing diagnostic and summary feedback on learning-to-learn capacities for use by students and faculty

In general, assessment focused on learning outcomes helps students learn to evaluate their own growth — a key learning-to-learn skill. Chapter 9 suggests ways to include learning to learn in assessment.

1.3.3 Faculty Concerns about Assessment

Faculty frequently express concerns about assessment. They wonder, legitimately, how the data will be used. They doubt that important outcomes can be quantified. They are uncertain whether they have the expertise, time, or inclination to become engaged in assessment. In a recent survey of accounting faculty, virtually all respondents in schools where assessment is currently "under discussion" rated instrument selection a major concern. About 75% rated "developing faculty motivation and participation" as a major problem (FSA Task Force on Assessment, in preparation).

Surveys and interviews of faculty and students also indicate that creating a positive environment for assessment is viewed as a major challenge facing those responsible. Curricular change is "labor intensive, requiring an inordinate time commitment" with few rewards. Faculty may "lack confidence in teaching new and unknown competencies." Both faculty and students fear that innovative programs will fail to prepare students for the content-heavy CPA exam (Pincus, Scott, Searfoss, and Clark, 1993).

Faculty may also be concerned that assessment will be used to force the acceptance of a single, rigid model of the accounting program. Administrators responsible for initiating assessment can point to the diverse range of curricular approaches and assessment methods in AECC grant-funded programs to counteract this concern. The *Objectives* should be understood as a broad set of principles rather than as the blueprint for a monolithic approach to accounting education. Assessment can, in fact, promote creativity by inspiring confidence in the choices made by faculty to improve learning.

Faculty may well resist an assessment program imposed (or perceived as imposed) from the "top down," particularly if the purpose and value of the program are not made clear. They will also resist a program whose results may be used to judge the effectiveness of individual faculty members. In an ideal environment, faculty are willing to undertake educational experiments, to seek and respond to feedback from students and other stakeholders, and to engage in open discussion of educational matters. In turn, administrators must be fair and open about the uses of assessment data, and willing to reward faculty participation in curricular change and assessment.

Once an assessment program is underway, some concerns may be reduced. For example, only one-third of respondents in schools "currently operating a program to assess student learning and development" felt faculty motivation was a major concern and instrument selection is viewed as problematic by faculty actively involved in assessment (FSA Task Force on Assessment, in preparation).

A wise administrator will recognize and seek to address the concerns of both faculty and students. Faculty must have reason to believe that the benefits of assessment will outweigh the costs. They must see their investment in curriculum development and assessment as leading to tangible program improvement. Incentives and rewards for faculty participation in assessment must be developed to initiate and sustain a serious effort. Currently, the reward structure at many institutions is neutral or negative toward such participation, although nationally, a focus on curriculum, instruction, and assessment is increasingly recognized as essential for educational quality (e.g., *Change,* July/August 1993; Boyer, 1990).

Faculty concerns may also be addressed by building trust through continuous, open communication about the program. Informal seminars may alleviate faculty concerns by:

- Creating a forum for open discussion of the issues
- Describing a continuum of assessment practices
- Exploring ways in which the faculty themselves currently use assessment in teaching and program review

Briefings on assessment projects should be included on the agenda at departmental meetings. Members of the assessment committee should also meet informally with faculty individually or in small groups to facilitate two-way communication about assessment.

Concerns may be further reduced by adopting guidelines for good practice such as those presented in Figure 1.1. These principles suggest issues for faculty to consider as they develop their own guidelines for assessment. The original document, available from AAHE, presents a brief explanation of each principle. Each is reflected in various ways throughout this guide, as indicated by the chapter references in parentheses in Figure 1.1.

FIGURE 1.1
PRINCIPLES OF GOOD PRACTICE FOR ASSESSING STUDENT LEARNING
AAHE Assessment Forum
(1992, pp. 2-3)

- The assessment of student learning begins with educational values (Introduction, Chapters 4, 6, and 7).
- Assessment is most effective when it reflects an understanding of learning as multidimensional, integrated, and revealed in performance over time (Chapters 3 and 8).
- Assessment works best when the programs it seeks to improve have clear, explicitly stated purposes (Chapters 5 and 6).
- Assessment requires attention to outcomes but also and equally to the experiences that lead to those outcomes (Chapters 9 and 10).
- Assessment works best when it is ongoing, not episodic (Chapters 3 and 8).
- Assessment fosters wider improvement when representatives from across the educational community are involved (Chapters 2 and 9).
- Assessment makes a difference when it begins with issues of use and illuminates questions that people really care about (Introduction, Chapter 4).
- Assessment is most likely to lead to improvement when it is part of a larger set of conditions that promote change (Chapters 1, 2, and 4).
- Through assessment, educators meet responsibilities to students and to the public (Chapter 1 and throughout this guide).

Chapter 2
STAKEHOLDERS AND PARTICIPANTS
IN ASSESSMENT

This chapter identifies roles and responsibilities of key stakeholders and participants in the assessment process:

- Faculty and Administrators
- Assessment Committee Members
- Employers and other Program Constituents

2.1 Faculty and Administrators: Joint Responsibility for Assessment

Principal responsibility for successful assessment, as for curriculum and instruction, rests with the faculty. Just as faculty expertise stimulates the curriculum, so should the department's information needs motivate the design of assessment. Assessment requires agreement about curricular goals and priorities, how improvement will be measured, and how results will be interpreted and used. To ensure acceptance of the process and results, key faculty should be given leadership roles.

Faculty involvement in assessment, however, is only part of the equation. Administrators have a responsibility to ensure that a systematic program of assessment is developed, and that faculty contributions will be well supported by the department and school. The department chair and/or dean must provide the resources and incentives to keep assessment high on the agenda. They must encourage collaboration and see to it that assessment becomes an integral part of departmental planning. Because faculty and administrators share responsibility for assessment, they must agree on key issues such as the following:

- Who will implement assessment?
- What are the specific purposes and priorities of the assessment program?
- How will resources and time for assessment be allocated?
- How will findings be used to improve the curriculum and instruction?
- What are appropriate incentives and rewards for participation in assessment?
- Who will review and update the assessment program?

Many other groups and individuals have a stake in the curriculum and the results of assessment as well. Their roles and interests are discussed in Section 2.3.

2.2 Role of the Assessment Committee

Once the decision has been made to formalize assessment, the department chair or dean, in consultation with members of the department or school, should locate responsibility for assessment clearly within the department. One option is to establish a faculty committee and a coordinator, with at least one member who is also a member of the departmental curriculum committee. The discussion that follows assumes that a committee structure exists.

To ensure the program's credibility from the outset, the assessment committee should include faculty who have an interest in assessment and who are well respected within the department and the profession. Faculty who express reservations should not be excluded but drawn into the process so that their concerns can be addressed. Faculty who are asked to take leadership roles should have a clear understanding, preferably in writing, about how their participation will influence evaluation of their performance.

The committee will not necessarily implement the assessment; rather, it may facilitate the process and serve in a resource capacity. Initially, the committee should gather information and clarify curricular goals. If the department does not have a clearly articulated set of curricular goals, members of the committee should work with the curriculum committee to specify key competencies required for program graduates. Identifying these goals is essential to the development of an assessment program, since the goals determine what is to be evaluated (see Chapters 4 and 6 for details).

The assessment committee should also inventory existing data sources on students, program characteristics, and learning outcomes. Most institutions collect data on students, some of which can be useful for program-level assessment. Commonly available data sources include admission and alumni records, attrition/retention data, current student and alumni surveys conducted by the institutional research office (which can often be analyzed by school if not by major), grade distribution reports, transcripts, and so on.

By focusing initially on acquiring background knowledge and inventorying locally available data, the committee establishes a pattern of faculty involvement while providing a sound foundation for further development of the program. By reporting regularly to the department from the beginning, the committee gains important feedback on its direction. Regular reports also build interest in curricular questions, and build faculty ownership as the program progresses.

The assessment committee may organize into subcommittees charged with responsibility for studying specific curricular goals. For example, one subcommittee might focus on objectives related to critical thinking and problem solving, while another might focus on those related to a systems perspective. The committee should also meet frequently as a whole to coordinate the project.

Possible responsibilities of the assessment committee include the following:

- Information Gathering
  - Become familiar with assessment practice in general and in accounting in particular
  - Gather resources, bibliographic materials and examples of assessment materials
  - Determine instruments already in use by faculty
  - Consult faculty colleagues, staff, and outside experts with relevant expertise
- Consultation and Planning
  - Engage faculty, students, and other stakeholders in clarifying program outcomes
  - Consult regularly with the faculty, department chair/dean, and key stakeholders
  - Determine the applicability of available measurement tools
- Implementation/Oversight
  - Assist with development and implementation of assessment plans
  - Compile results with assistance of faculty and others involved

- Communication
  - Routinely report to faculty and chair on progress of the assessment program
  - Organize the distribution, discussion, and use of assessment results
  - Review effectiveness of the assessment program and recommend changes
  - Evaluate resource allocation for assessment

2.3 Involving Others in Assessment

Faculty must design and implement both the curriculum and the interrelated assessment program. Many others, however, also have a stake in the process and its results. They, too, should be consulted throughout the design process.

Key stakeholders and possible roles in assessment include:

- Central Administration
  - Academic administrators above the level of dean should support development and implementation of the assessment program.
- Department Chair and Dean
  - As noted above, administrators share responsibility with faculty for assessment. In consultation with faculty, the chair or dean will generally appoint the assessment committee. Administrators initiate, facilitate, and monitor progress of the assessment committee. They simplify distribution and discussion of results, and support recommendations.
- Students
  - Students are important stakeholders who can assist in identifying questions for assessment, as well as completing surveys, interviews, and outcome measures. Students also provide feedback on assessment and should assist in interpretation of results.
- Program Advisory Boards
  - A program advisory board (including members of the business community) can participate in developing or reviewing the overall design for assessment. A board can help identify benchmarks for professional competencies of graduates and advise faculty of competencies expected of graduates at different times in their careers.
- Alumni
  - Alumni can assist by helping to identify questions for assessment, by participating in surveys, interviews and focus groups, and by assisting in interpretation of results.
- Support Staff (e.g., librarians, instructional development staff, academic computing staff, institutional research officer)
  - Support staff can provide needed resources and expertise for assessment design and implementation.
- Employers and Internship Supervisors
  - Employers can assist in identifying questions for assessment, participate in surveys and interviews, and evaluate students' and graduates' performance.

Students are especially important constituents whose concerns and expectations should not be overlooked. With the new emphasis on "learning to learn," they will encounter methods of instruction and evaluation that may be unfamiliar or at least unexpected in the context of professional accounting. An orientation may be necessary to expose students' concerns, increase their understanding of the program, and clarify faculty expectations. In addition, within each course faculty can state course objectives clearly in the syllabus and explain how these objectives relate to instructional methods, evaluation, grading, and program goals.

Dialogue and collaboration with representatives of these groups can help faculty clarify program goals and refine assessment procedures. Inclusion of constituent voices in the planning stages of a new curriculum and its assessment will also increase understanding of the program and generate goodwill for the sponsoring department.

Chapter 3
A MODEL FOR ASSESSMENT PLANNING

This chapter summarizes the model for assessment planning and implementation described in the remaining chapters. The model is represented visually in the icon used throughout the document. Examples of assessment plans are presented in Tables 3.1 and 3.2.

Assessment planning can be conceptualized in terms of eight essential components. A brief description and illustration of each follows.

PROCESS	ILLUSTRATION
Establish Assessment Purposes and Priorities: The assessment committee must specify the planning processes and decisions the assessment will support. The primary purpose of assessment is to improve learning outcomes. Assessment also serves multiple purposes, such as increasing program focus, marketing the program, and ensuring public accountability.	*Provide information to support curricular and instructional planning related to student learning outcomes in three areas: communication skills, teamwork, and professional ethics.*
Establish Budget and Obtain Needed Resources: Allocation of adequate resources is crucial to realize benefits of assessment. The assessment committee should identify needed resources and work with the administration to obtain them. The committee should seek to minimize costs and maximize benefits by capitalizing on existing data sources. The budget should answer the question: What will the program cost?	*Costs for assessment include faculty participation, staff support, training and materials. Specific cost sources include planning, preparation and distribution of materials, data collection and analysis, and dissemination of results for discussion and use.*
Clarify Curricular Goals: Assessment compares actual outcomes to the goals of the curriculum to determine program effectiveness. The assessment committee must therefore review curricular goals to clarify intended outcomes of the academic program. The goals should reflect the institutional and departmental mission, and	*(Focus on communication skills):* "*Program graduates will be able to communicate effectively in professional settings, both orally and in writing.*"

the needs of the profession. They should answer the question: What is the program intended to accomplish?

Translate Goals into Curricular Objectives: The committee must translate educational goals into tangible outcomes or *objectives* so that appropriate measures can be designed or selected. Learning objectives at the program level can be identified through a review of program documents, curricular materials, course syllabi and exams, and actual student work. The objectives answer the question: What will program graduates be able to *do* as a consequence of their education?

Graduating seniors will be able to write or present a management report with a clear main point, using relevant examples and graphic illustrations to support their position.

Develop Research Plan and Methodology: The assessment research plan specifies questions to be investigated, key variables and measures to assess them, data collection procedures, groups to be studied, sample sizes, and analytical methods. The plan should yield credible information of practical significance and interest to faculty. The research plan answers the question: What do we want to find out, and how will we go about it? What should we measure? What methodology should be used?

Research question #1: Do students' communication skills improve from sophomore to senior year? What factors influence change? Method: *Communication skills and related learning experiences will be assessed in sophomore, junior, and senior years; trend analysis and causal modeling will be used to monitor changes and determine contributing factors.*

Research question #2: Do graduating seniors display communication skills to meet the demands of practice? Method: *Practicing professionals will review a sample of videotaped senior presentations, then participate in a focus group to discuss students' readiness to communicate effectively in professional practice, identify additional needs, and offer feedback to individual students.*

Develop Measures to Assess Learning Outcomes: This part of the assessment plan describes the measures that will be used to evaluate learning outcomes. *Cognitive outcomes* such as communication skills and ethical reasoning can often be measured using "authentic" methods (such as oral presentations, simulations, and portfolios

Videotaped presentations by students will be rated by faculty and practicing professionals on selection and application of accounting principles, complex problem solving, and communication skills.

of student work) embedded in classroom instruction. A single measure can often be used to assess several different learning outcomes. *Multiple* measures should be used to validate results, especially for high-priority outcomes.

Values and attitudes are measured using questionnaires, surveys, interviews, focus groups, unobtrusive observations, simulations, and rating forms. The measures chosen should help to answer the question: What student behavior will we examine to determine whether the outcomes have been attained?

Develop Measures to Assess Contributions of the Educational Environment: The e*ducational environment* can be measured by observation, student and alumni perceptions and satisfaction ratings, review of program documents and instructional materials, and review of institutional records on matters such as persistence, attrition, and course-taking patterns. The measures selected should help to answer the question: What factors in the educational environment should we examine to understand influences on learning outcomes?

To assess factors in the educational environment related to communication and other skills, a faculty subcommittee will construct a matrix indicating which courses address these skills through a) instruction, and b) evaluation. They will review instructional materials and student and alumni perception of instruction related to these skills.

Use Results for Program Improvement: Prior to implementing its program, the assessment committee should specify the format, timing, and context for reporting results to stakeholders as well as how the data will be used for improvement of learning outcomes and processes. The plan for reporting results should be based on the original statement of purposes and priorities for assessment. The plan should answer the question: How will results influence the accounting curriculum and teaching methodology?

At a departmental meeting or retreat, the assessment committee will present results of three assessment initiatives described above (focus groups or videotaped student presentations, review of instructional materials, and student and alumni evaluations). The faculty will interpret results and recommend changes if warranted.

Identify Process Improvements: The assessment committee and department chair should review the assessment program or assign responsibility elsewhere. Review criteria should include accuracy, relevance, usefulness of the process and results, cost-effectiveness, and benefit to students. The committee should identify ways to improve and simplify the process and to increase the value and use of results. The process should answer the question: How will what we have learned from this cycle affect the curriculum and what have we learned to improve cycles in the future?

The department chair, dean, and assessment committee will analyze costs and benefits of the program at the end of each year of implementation, and make recommendations to the faculty at a department meeting.

TABLE 3.1

SAMPLE DEPARTMENT ASSESSMENT PLAN A

The following assessment activities will be phased in over a 5-year period.

Goal	Objective: Students will be able to:	Assessment Measures	Time Frame	Use of Results
Professional knowledge as foundation for lifelong learning	Apply and adapt accounting concepts and principles in a variety of contexts and circumstances (*Objectives*, p. 6)	Portfolio analysis: Faculty judgments of students' use of accounting knowledge based on portfolio of major assignments and Senior Capstone Project	Junior and senior year	Determine patterns of strength and weakness in junior year; use to advise individual students, identify curricular needs for senior year and/or future sophomore-junior instruction
Information Management Skills	Access, organize and synthesize information from print and electronic sources	Faculty judgment of information skills, included as a rating scale on relevant class projects	Junior and senior year	Same as above
Critical Thinking Skills	Use correct inference and deduction, recognize assumptions, interpret evidence, and evaluate arguments	Diagnostic critical thinking skills test Faculty judgments of students' reasoning, using holistic rating scale when grading targeted projects	Sophomore year Junior year	Annually compile holistic ratings for each class of students; review for trends, identify needed improvements if indicated
Communication Skills	Use verbal and graphic displays effectively to communicate financial information and recommendations	Samples drawn from coursework	Annual review of representative sample of student presentations	Sophomore-senior comparison to determine growth; senior year review by practicing professionals
Attitude of Continual Inquiry and Lifelong Learning	[Graduates will] continue their professional education throughout their careers	Alumni Surveys Employer Surveys	Every 3-5 years	Review annually; monitor trends; identify concerns
Satisfaction with Learning Environment	[Alumni will] express satisfaction with their professional preparation and suggest improvements based on changing needs of the profession	Alumni Survey	Two, five, and ten years after graduation	Review survey results; identify issues and recommended changes as needed

TABLE 3.2
SAMPLE DEPARTMENT ASSESSMENT PLAN B

I. Essential Goals of the Curriculum
    A. Adaptable Professional Knowledge
    B. Effective Communication
    C. Problem Solving
    D. Learning to Learn
    E. Professional Integrity

II. Assessment Strategies and Uses
    A. Curricular Map (start-up plus review every two years)
        1. Faculty report instructional emphasis for each major goal; assistant compiles into a curricular map
        2. Map is reviewed to identify gaps and overlap
        3. Faculty agree on ways to improve balance of curricular emphasis

    B. Faculty Ratings of Student Performance (start-up plus review after 1 year of use)
        1. Faculty formulate objectives and performance criteria for all essential goals.
        2. Faculty develop rating scales for each major goal.
        3. Each faculty member agrees to use at least two of the rating scales to grade at least 3 major assignments each year.

    C. Portfolios of Student Work (annually)
        1. At the start of each year, faculty identify major projects that students will include in the portfolio.
        2. At the end of each year, students turn in portfolios for departmental review.
        3. Faculty review a selected sample to identify strengths and weaknesses in students' approach and clarify differences between students who receive grades at each level
            a. Qualitative assessment of a stratified sample of portfolios: for example, 5 each from students who received A, B, C, and D grades
            b. Quantitative analysis using compiled ratings of all students on assignments identified in B.3.
        4. Faculty use results to review objectives, identify strengths and/or needed changes, and familiarize themselves with work done by students in courses prerequisite to their own.
        5. Each fall, faculty return portfolios; students submit "best-effort" portfolio, 3 items to be used for advising, recommendations, etc.

    D. Learning Styles Assessment (start of each academic year, new students only)
        1. Entering students complete Nelson's Accounting Attitude Scale and Myers-Briggs through Counseling Center and receive a copy of results (with individual or group consultation if available).
        2. Profile of results is compiled and distributed to faculty
        3. Implications of profiles and individual differences are discussed with students in a special session
        4. Faculty discuss instructional implications and adjust methods to both challenge and support students
        5. At end of year, juniors complete Accounting Attitude Scale for sophomore-junior comparison

    E. Surveys (one per year)
        1. Faculty adapt surveys from other institutions to reflect program goals
        2. Surveys are administered to a different group each year:
            a. Alumni
            b. Current Juniors
            c. Graduating Seniors
            d. Employers/recruiters
        3. Faculty identify implications and recommendations for follow-up.

III. Implementation Strategy
    A. Each member of the assessment committee takes the lead on one of the five methods.
    B. Each one also takes lead responsibility for one of the five goals.
    C. Committee meets periodically and reports at least quarterly at department meetings.
    D. Recommendations are developed jointly by members of the department.
    E. Responsibility for implementation and follow-up assessment is assigned as appropriate.

PART II
DEVELOPING THE ASSESSMENT PROGRAM

Assessment for improvement begins not with an instrument but with a question.
(Ewell, 1994, p. 21)

CHAPTER 4

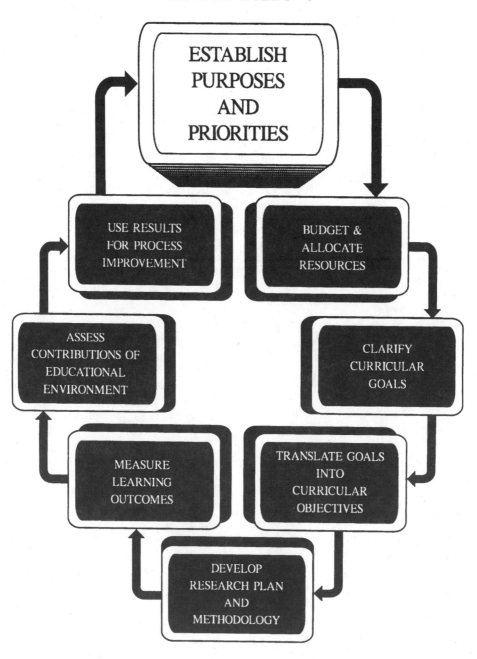

ESTABLISH
PURPOSES
AND
PRIORITIES

USE RESULTS
FOR PROCESS
IMPROVEMENT

BUDGET &
ALLOCATE
RESOURCES

ASSESS
CONTRIBUTIONS OF
EDUCATIONAL
ENVIRONMENT

CLARIFY
CURRICULAR
GOALS

MEASURE
LEARNING
OUTCOMES

TRANSLATE GOALS
INTO
CURRICULAR
OBJECTIVES

DEVELOP
RESEARCH PLAN
AND
METHODOLOGY

Chapter 4
ESTABLISHING PURPOSES AND PRIORITIES
OF ASSESSMENT

Because assessment requires a considerable investment of time and fiscal resources, the faculty and responsible administrators should carefully consider *why* the department is initiating or developing an assessment program. Although administrative request (or even mandate) is in some cases the initial motivating force, it is the department's responsibility to decide what specific purposes the assessment should serve, and what priorities should guide implementation.

Table 4.1 illustrates a worksheet to be completed by stakeholders and then used for discussion of assessment priorities.

4.1 Primary Purpose: Obtaining Information for Educational Decision Making

From a quality standpoint, the primary purpose of assessment is providing information to improve learning outcomes and client satisfaction. Feedback to individual students and faculty is important, but it is *not* the primary purpose of program-level assessment.

Assessment answers a variety of questions about the academic program. This document focuses primarily on understanding what students learn and how their learning can be improved:

- How do our students' skills improve as they advance in the program?
- How do our graduates measure up to employers' expectations and needs?
- What effect does our program have on students with various characteristics?
- How can our program be improved?
- What changes will most benefit specific subgroups of students?

4.2 Secondary Purpose: Obtaining Information for Accountability

Assessment findings may also be used to inform key constituencies about program effectiveness, for example, program reviewers, accreditation representatives, or potential employers. The assessment program thus helps the department:

- Prepare for self-study for pending accreditation
- Strengthen its program review cycle
- Document program quality to attract better students
- Document results to meet external demands for accountability
- Gain credibility and ensure public funding by demonstrating return on investment
- Enhance program profile to attract private funds

Having a good assessment program *itself* is an indicator of quality, suggesting that the department has a philosophy of continuous improvement.

4.3 Establishing Assessment Priorities

Attempting a comprehensive assessment all at once is an overwhelming task. Instead, priorities should balance areas of immediate concern with longer-range information needs. The assessment committee's review of program documents will reveal valued features or goals of the program that warrant careful evaluation. The committee can further clarify priorities through discussions among the faculty and with students, alumni, and potential employers. By selecting areas of interest to stakeholders, the committee increases the incentive to obtain and use assessment results.

Priorities may be determined by identifying:

- Program distinctiveness
- Significant recent changes (for example, curricular or pedagogical innovations)
- Student groups whose rate of attrition is unexpectedly high or low
- Concerns frequently voiced by students, faculty, and/or employers

Selecting one or two high-priority areas enables the faculty to develop a balanced, multi-dimensional portfolio to address strategic interests of the department. For example, the faculty may set a high priority on the ability to adapt to new technologies. The assessment should therefore help faculty identify students' current abilities, current curricular emphasis, and ways to strengthen technological adaptability. Section 4.5 illustrates the translation of assessment purposes and priorities into specific assessment objectives and methods.

Results of the assessment should be shared with students as well as faculty to foster open discussion of program strengths, weaknesses, and strategies for improvement. Reporting and use of results are discussed in Chapter 11.

4.4 Using Priorities to Establish a Timetable for Assessment

When determining priorities for assessment, the committee should consider:

- Faculty interest and motivation to obtain information
- The value of early success on a high-quality pilot project that provides useful information
- The need to build faculty experience with assessments
- The time and energy required to develop a useful assessment portfolio
- The rhythms of the academic year

The assessment committee may wish to consider a cyclic plan in which some objectives are assessed every year, others every few years. Assessment of high-priority areas should be the focus in the first year or two of the program, with additional priorities added when questions about these areas are resolved and their assessment becomes more routine and/or less frequent. Periodic review of the assessment program, described in Chapter 12, will reveal areas where its scope can be reduced, for example, when a new program initiative has become fully institutionalized.

The assessment committee may wish to set goals for the program itself, for example, to obtain information on at least two significant learning outcomes of the accounting program, or to evaluate satisfaction with the program as reported by at least one significant constituent group each year.

4.5 Translating Purposes of Assessment into Assessment Objectives and Methods

Questions about learning outcomes can be addressed through studies of:

- Knowledge, skills and professional orientation acquired by students
- Trends in students' mastery of curricular goals from year to year
- The influence of specific program components on learning outcomes
- Student, faculty, alumni, and employer perceptions of the program
- Employer perceptions of graduates' strengths and weaknesses

The examples below illustrate multi-faceted approaches to achievement of specific assessment purposes.

Purpose #1: Improve the accounting program by increasing consistency of outcomes across all sections of the elementary course in accordance with AECC's Position Statement on "The First Course in Accounting" (Position Statement No. 2).
Assessment Objective: Clarify current focus of the introductory course and analyze students' achievements in light of AECC goals. Use findings to negotiate consensus on major objectives. Monitor progress after changes are implemented.
Possible Methods: Examine instructional materials and portfolios of student work selected from the first course to clarify current areas of emphasis. Use focus groups to obtain faculty and students' perceptions and suggestions for change. After refining goals and implementing changes, track quality and consistency of learning outcomes, and performance in subsequent courses.

Purpose #2: Improve program quality by strengthening students' knowledge of technological innovations, skill in using current technology, and ability to learn new technologies quickly.
Assessment Objectives: Identify employer needs related to technology and their perceptions of graduates' technological skills. Assess students' technological skills.
Possible Methods: Conduct employer surveys and/or focus groups; distribute questionnaires to obtain students' self-ratings on technological knowledge, skills, and confidence in learning new technologies. Plan changes and monitor impact.

Purpose #3: Improve sequencing of curricular content.
Assessment Objective: Identify redundancies and gaps in the curriculum to improve sequencing while reducing unnecessary overlap in course content.
Possible Methods: Administer pre-tests to check prior learning/retention. Analyze predictive value of grades in prerequisite courses. Plan changes and track results.

Purpose #4: Improve student performance and reduce attrition at the entry level, particularly among women and students of color.
Assessment Objective: Identify possible sources of attrition.
Possible Methods: Compare characteristics of students who withdraw or fail to those who succeed. Verify completion and performance in courses completed. Use focus groups to obtain students' views of classroom/program climate and instructional methods. Consult campus instructional improvement staff to analyze sources of difficulty and develop solutions. Implement changes and track results.

Purpose #5: Determine whether ethical issues should receive greater emphasis in the curriculum.

Assessment Objective: Determine current emphasis on ethics and values in the curriculum. Assess students' knowledge and ability to apply ethical concepts in case discussions, and in their professional lives.

Possible Methods: Review ethics coverage in specific courses; conduct in-class simulations or a pilot study using focus groups to determine students' ethical decision-making skills and awareness of professional ethics and values (for example, see Dirsmith and Ketz, 1987; Ponemon, 1993). Consult with employers and alumni. If gaps or deficiencies exist, develop and implement changes and monitor results.

4.6 The Broader Purpose of Assessment: Assessing Vitality and Excellence

Regardless of the pragmatic purpose for which assessment is designed, the process can also serve a broader purpose in terms of faculty and curricular vitality. De Mong, Lindgren, and Perry report that "The assessment program may increase teamwork among faculty, causing them to view their contribution to the program as a whole and not in terms of an isolated course or area." (1994, p. 14) Acknowledging that assessment is time-consuming, they comment based on their experience in the McIntire School of Commerce at the University of Virginia that the assessment program has benefitted the department in two ways:

> *First,* it has forced us to define our expectations for our students. Once we had defined our expectations, we were able to focus our study and evaluation of the curriculum proposals on our common goals. *Second,* the assessment program has provided a true feedback loop for our accounting program. We were able to enjoy our successes and develop strategies to overcome our weaknesses. As our experience with assessment accumulates, we expect even greater rewards. (1994, p. 26)

Assessment turns faculty attention to the curriculum, instruction, and students' needs as learners and future professionals. It provides an empirical foundation for discussions of issues central to the educational process. Whatever purposes, objectives and methods are selected, the role of assessment in fostering a departmental culture centered on excellence should not be overlooked.

TABLE 4.1
WORKSHEET:
STAKEHOLDERS AND PURPOSES OF ASSESSMENT

PURPOSES:

STAKEHOLDERS:	Monitor Health of Program	Guide Planning & Improvement Efforts	Attract Better/Different Students	Provide Info Relevant to Policies/Decisions	Attract Resources	Increase Accountability
Faculty	[ ]	[ ]	[ ]	[ ]	[ ]	[ ]
Students	[ ]	[ ]	[ ]	[ ]	[ ]	[ ]
Employers	[ ]	[ ]	[ ]	[ ]	[ ]	[ ]
Alumni	[ ]	[ ]	[ ]	[ ]	[ ]	[ ]
Potential Donors	[ ]	[ ]	[ ]	[ ]	[ ]	[ ]
Trustees	[ ]	[ ]	[ ]	[ ]	[ ]	[ ]
Legislators	[ ]	[ ]	[ ]	[ ]	[ ]	[ ]
Business Community	[ ]	[ ]	[ ]	[ ]	[ ]	[ ]
Accounting Associations	[ ]	[ ]	[ ]	[ ]	[ ]	[ ]
Other Accounting Programs	[ ]	[ ]	[ ]	[ ]	[ ]	[ ]

DIRECTIONS: Rate the importance of each item for each stakeholder using the scale below. Collect ratings from various constituencies to assist in determining priorities for assessment.

1 = VERY IMPORTANT   2 = MODERATELY IMPORTANT   3 = UNIMPORTANT

Adapted from Southern Regional Education Board, "Benchmark Criteria." Gaile Gaines, 1992. Reprinted in "Developing a Report Card: A Summary of Research and Practices." KPMG Peat Marwick, September 1993, p. 4.

CHAPTER 5

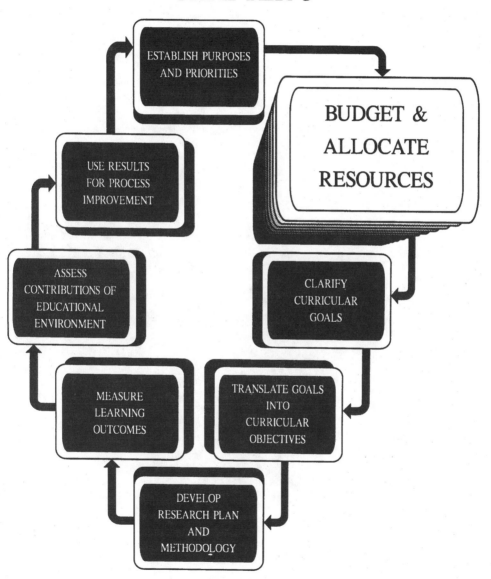

ESTABLISH PURPOSES AND PRIORITIES

BUDGET & ALLOCATE RESOURCES

USE RESULTS FOR PROCESS IMPROVEMENT

CLARIFY CURRICULAR GOALS

ASSESS CONTRIBUTIONS OF EDUCATIONAL ENVIRONMENT

MEASURE LEARNING OUTCOMES

TRANSLATE GOALS INTO CURRICULAR OBJECTIVES

DEVELOP RESEARCH PLAN AND METHODOLOGY

Chapter 5
BUDGETING AND ALLOCATING RESOURCES
FOR ASSESSMENT

Developing a budget and allocating resources is essential both to establish a realistic scope for assessment and to evaluate the cost/benefit ratio of the assessment program. Identification of costs should also help to clarify the focus of the assessment program. This chapter:

- Points out costs likely to be associated with assessment
- Discusses responsibilities of administrators and the assessment committee with respect to budgeting and allocating resources

5.1 Costs of Assessment

Costs for assessment include instruments, administration, data analysis, coordination and start-up costs (Ewell and Jones, 1986):

- *Instrument costs* include the purchase or development and validation of instruments. When performance assessments are used, faculty participation in rater training sessions may be a significant cost factor.
- *Administrative costs* are those associated with conducting procedures. They include supervising the assessment or mailing instruments, handling and storing data, and the opportunity costs for faculty and others involved.
- *Analysis costs* are those associated with faculty and other personnel needed to score and analyze the data.
- *Coordination costs* include keeping track of data from multiple sources and facilitating analysis through the efficient use of management information systems.
- *Start-up costs* include costs to educate faculty about assessment, to retain consultant services, to compile a centralized database, and to conduct pilot studies. Incentives and rewards for faculty who take leadership roles in the project may also be a substantial cost.

Some costs, such as those associated with clarifying curricular objectives, fall in the domain of curriculum development and should *not* be charged to assessment.

Frequently, the costs of assessment are limited to operating expenses, while overhead and opportunity costs are neglected. A full-cost budget may be contentious, but it provides crucial information for weighing the benefits of assessment. Conversely, when analyzing benefits, intangibles such as increased curricular coherence, improved qualification of graduates, and program reputation should be factored into the equation, along with more tangible outcomes such as graduates' employability and success.

5.2 Administrative Responsibility

Primary responsibility for allocation of resources belongs to the administration. Working with the assessment committee, the dean or department chair should establish an ongoing budget to ensure that necessary resources are always available. The budget should be reviewed and revised as part of *process improvement*, discussed in Chapter 11.

5.3 Assessment Committee Responsibility

To minimize costs, the assessment committee should (Ewell and Jones, 1986; Terenzini, 1989):

- *Focus on high-priority areas of the curriculum.* The assessment program should be limited in scope. Placing "the primary weight upon a particular dimension that matches the institution's unique curriculum and mission" (Ewell and Jones, 1986, p. 45) increases the likelihood that results will be used and costs will stay within limits.
- *Use existing data when possible.* This is accomplished by coordinating with the institutional research office, which may already survey current students, graduating seniors, withdrawing students, and/or alumni. These surveys frequently include questions about the major and other aspects of the students' educational experience. In some cases, they can be amended to include questions about learning outcomes in the major.
- *Use regularly assigned coursework as a source of data.* This method, referred to as "course-embedded" or "curriculum-embedded assessment" (Loacker et al., 1984; Farmer, 1988) uses coursework targeted to specific objectives, then evaluates it using departmental performance criteria. Investment in developing instruments and training faculty to use them consistently (discussed in detail in Chapter 9) will pay off in the long run. It will increase consistency of course-level evaluation and make it possible to aggregate or compare evaluation results for particular competencies across courses and assignments. Course-embedded assessment is also more motivating for students because they receive immediate feedback on their performance. This approach is less costly and more educationally useful than attempting a large-scale evaluation of complex abilities using a one-shot instrument.
- *Use inexpensive alternatives part of the time.* It may be possible, for example, to validate student self-report data against performance measures, then use frequent self-reports in combination with less frequent performance assessment of representative samples of students.
- *Consolidate and coordinate record-keeping.* A department database for student records allows centralized data analysis. These records should include course-embedded assessments as well as standardized test scores and other student data. A centralized database minimizes duplication of effort and encourages collaborative and exploratory studies.

Even with careful marshalling of resources, substantial funding will be required to maintain an assessment program involving multiple evaluations over an extended time period. Both technical and human costs must be factored into the budget.

CHAPTER 6

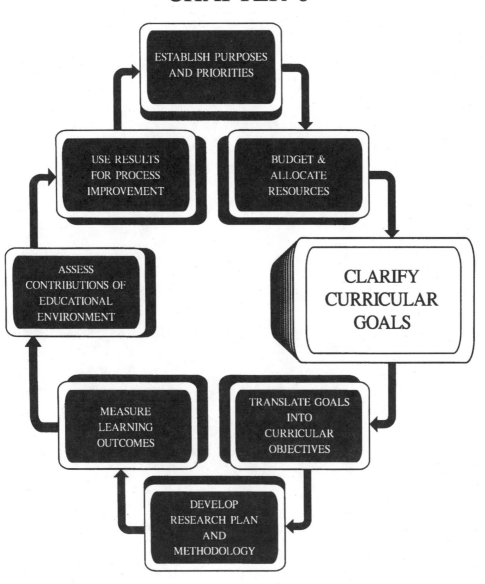

ESTABLISH PURPOSES
AND PRIORITIES

USE RESULTS
FOR PROCESS
IMPROVEMENT

BUDGET &
ALLOCATE
RESOURCES

ASSESS
CONTRIBUTIONS OF
EDUCATIONAL
ENVIRONMENT

CLARIFY
CURRICULAR
GOALS

MEASURE
LEARNING
OUTCOMES

TRANSLATE GOALS
INTO
CURRICULAR
OBJECTIVES

DEVELOP
RESEARCH PLAN
AND
METHODOLOGY

Chapter 6
CLARIFYING CURRICULAR GOALS

Clarifying curricular goals and translating them into learning objectives are key steps in preparing for assessment. This chapter:

- Defines and distinguishes between "goals" and "objectives"
- Suggests sources for identifying essential curricular goals
- Suggests the value of clarifying curricular goals
- Outlines major categories of curricular goals and objectives

Chapter 7 describes the development of objectives and performance criteria.

6.1 Goals and Objectives: Definition of Terms and a Key Distinction

Curricular goals define in broad terms the knowledge, skills, values, and attitudes faculty members believe will enable graduates to succeed as practicing professionals. The goals should be consistent with the mission of the university and school, and should encompass the expanded learning outcomes advocated by the AECC and other accounting organizations. Achieving clarity and consensus on program goals is a major challenge posed by assessment, with benefits for the entire academic program.

Curricular goals are stated in general terms, such as analytical reasoning, electronic information skills, interpersonal effectiveness, or professional integrity. Goals for student learning outcomes in accounting are sometimes referred to as "competencies."

Sample Goal (Communication): Program graduates will be able to communicate effectively in professional situations.

Objectives, in contrast, describe what students must do to demonstrate proficiency in a given area of concentration. Objectives translate curricular goals into descriptions of *performance*, operationally defined for use in curriculum development, teaching, evaluation of individual students, and program-level assessment. Because objectives emphasize what students can actually *do*, they are frequently referred to as "performance outcomes" or "behavioral objectives". While most programs state broad curricular goals, assessment requires the further specificity of objectives.

Sample Objective (Communication, high-level): Students will be able to present and convincingly support advice to a hypothetical client on future investment decisions. The presentation will be made either orally or in writing, to the satisfaction of an audience of faculty and/or practicing accountants.

The key difference is that objectives describe learning outcomes in terms of a student's *behavior* rather than a state of mind, which is often the focus of goals. A goal may call for evidence of students' *understanding* of a principle, which can only be *inferred* from behavior. For example, a goal related to auditing might state that students should "understand options for presenting accounting information in an audit." In contrast, the related *objectives* indicate *how* the student will demonstrate "understanding," for example, by stating that the student will be able to *evaluate* the options (high-level objective) or simply *list* and *explain* them (low-level objective). Levels of objectives are discussed in more detail in Section 6.4.

Translating goals into objectives is essential for movement from curricular ideals to knowledge of results in terms of students' performance in the classroom and the workplace. The process of operationally defining goals is described in Chapter 7.

6.2 Sources of Goals and Objectives for the Academic Program

The assessment and/or curriculum committee should consult both internal and external stakeholders when developing program goals and objectives. Faculty who have developed program goals in other professional contexts have found that:

> to ensure the acceptance of goals, all appropriate and interested parties should have the opportunity to participate in their development and/or revision. This will, at a minimum, include all faculty, but should also involve students and local practitioners or the appropriate professional societies. Other factors to be considered are the dean's vision, legislative directives, and institutional-level definitions (Romberg, 1990, p. 11).

The AECC and major professional associations have recommended expanded goals and objectives for accounting as it is evolving today. The AECC's *Objectives* identify competencies necessary for professional success, based on outcomes identified by major accounting firms in a paper entitled *Perspectives on Education: Capabilities for Success in the Accounting Profession* (Arthur Andersen & Co. and others, 1989), often referred to as the "Big Eight White Paper." Through the 1986 "Bedford Committee" Report, the AAA has proposed a similar framework (AAA Committee on the Future..., 1986). Goals such as those identified by the AECC are consistent with the goals of the AAA and AACSB, and standards of regional accreditation bodies. They are specific enough to be translated into measurable tasks with defined performance criteria, yet general enough to permit a wide range of educational approaches. These goal statements, in conjunction with course syllabi, program documents, and employer recommendations, are an important resource for faculty as they formulate goals and objectives representative of their school.

Not all goals and objectives identified in these sources are equally important to all employers. A review of performance appraisal forms used by employers of one university's graduates identified competencies from the "Bedford Report" (1986) and *Perspectives* (1989) which were actually used in supervisor evaluations. While employers considered many of the objectives stated in these documents, several were not evaluated at all. For example:

- No employer evaluated employees on objectives related to "Design and Use of Information Systems" or "Decision Problems and Information in Organizations."
- Of the four objectives related to "General Knowledge," only *experience in making value judgments* was assessed.

- Communication, intellectual, and interpersonal skills, however, *were* evaluated by these employers (Baker and others, 1993, pp. 43-44 and 52-55).

Information based on practice logs and surveys of CPAs is available in the AICPA's *Practice Analysis of Certified Public Accountants in Public Accounting* (Greenberg and Smith, 1991). Approximately 2000 AICPA members were surveyed; the sample was weighted toward early-career members to assist in improving the validity of the CPA licensure examination. The report identifies major tasks of practicing CPAs in accounting and auditing and in taxation.

The eight tasks identified for accounting and auditing are listed in Figure 6.1. For each task, the report identifies relevant activities, knowledge, and skills and presents CPAs' estimates of when those should be acquired (see, Greenberg and Smith, 1991, Appendix 13). This analysis of expert practice will help faculty identify knowledge and skills that graduates will find most useful in the early stages of their careers. The analysis may also suggest in-class activities, projects, examinations and evaluation criteria for use in the curriculum.

These studies provide guidance, but the assessment committee should validate goal statements for local use by surveying employers about what counts in their working environment.

6.3 Value of Clarifying Curricular Goals

Clear goals and consensus about priorities benefit the program above and beyond the immediate task of assessment planning. Clear goals:

- Convey a strong sense of direction and purpose within the program
- Facilitate communication with prospective and current students, employers, and the general public about performance expectations
- Help to attract students who are most likely to value what the program has to offer
- Facilitate increased program impact on student learning

Often, faculty discussion of program goals reveals significant agreement about their aspirations for graduates. In some instances, however, a lack of explicitly stated goals arises from disagreements (real or perceived) among faculty about what the program should accomplish. Open discussion of such disagreements is the first step toward clarifying program goals. Clarity and consensus about the goals lend direction and energy to build the future of the program.

6.4 Major Categories of Learning Outcomes

The learning outcomes prescribed by the AECC *Objectives* include both professional and general *knowledge, skills*, and *values and attitudes*. Goals and objectives that describe knowledge and skills are classified in the "cognitive" domain. Values and attitudes are classified in the "affective" domain (Bloom, 1956).

6.4.1 The Cognitive Domain: Knowledge and Skills

Goals and objectives in the cognitive domain are commonly divided into six types: knowledge, comprehension, application, analysis, synthesis, and evaluation. Referred to as Bloom's Taxonomy, this categorization system is summarized in Figure 6.2. Figure 6.2 also

---

FIGURE 6.1
ACCOUNTING AND AUDITING TASKS AND ACTIVITIES[1]

1.1 Evaluate client and engagement to determine whether to accept them.

1.2 Enter into agreement with client to achieve a mutual understanding of the terms of the engagement.

1.3 Plan the engagement to achieve its objectives and goals in an efficient and effective manner.

1.4 Obtain and document data to form a basis for conclusions.

1.5 Evaluate information to reach and document engagement conclusions.

1.6 Prepare communications to satisfy engagement objectives.

1.7 Perform engagement review to provide reasonable assurance that goals and objectives were achieved.

1.8 Communicate results to appropriate parties to fulfill terms of engagement.

---

[1]Adapted from Greenberg and Smith, 1991, pp. 319-321.

---

illustrates application of the taxonomy to outcomes in accounting, with specific reference to the use of accounting information in investment decision making.

The six levels of outcomes are frequently grouped into "lower-order" and "higher-order" outcomes, as follows:

Knowledge and *comprehension* outcomes, which require only recall, recognition, or explanation of concepts, are referred to as "lower-order" cognitive objectives. These objectives require students to demonstrate familiarity with essential concepts and principles but require minimal application, adaptation, or use of this knowledge. Assessment measures based on lower-order objectives generally require students to produce a single correct answer or follow an established procedure.

Application, analysis, synthesis, and *evaluation* are considered "higher-order" cognitive objectives. They combine *knowledge* and *skills* to specify *how* concepts, principles, procedures, and/or theories are to be used by the learner. Assessment measures based on higher-order objectives usually have no single correct answer and may even require students to identify the central problem or question (as in Harvard-style cases; Libby, 1991).

Higher-order objectives tap learning-to-learn skills such as those identified by Frances, Mulder, and Stark (in preparation): questioning, organizing, connecting, reflecting upon, and adapting knowledge for new purposes. Because achievement of higher-order objectives requires effective *use* of concepts and principles, it is possible to include knowledge and comprehension objectives *within* measures of higher-order objectives.

Extending beyond the traditional categories outlined by Bloom, the AECC and others have identified three specific categories of professional competence:

- *Intellectual skills,* for example, the ability to identify and solve unstructured problems in unfamiliar settings, to think critically, to manage challenging pressures and to identify and resolve ethical issues
- *Interpersonal skills,* for example, teamwork, leadership, and the ability to interact with culturally and intellectually diverse people
- *Communication skills,* such as the ability to listen effectively, to transfer and receive information with ease, and to present and support a position (AECC *Objectives,* 1990)

While Bloom's taxonomy emphasizes the application of knowledge, the AECC's categorization identifies a wide range of skills for professional practice.

6.4.2 The Affective Domain: Values and Attitudes

In addition to knowledge and skill outcomes, the faculty may wish to address professionally related values and attitudes, categorized in the "affective domain" by Bloom and others. The AECC *Objectives* specifies several outcomes related to graduates' professional orientation, including empathy, integrity, leadership, sensitivity to social responsibilities, and a commitment to lifelong learning. Professional ethics are increasingly a focus of accounting and other business programs.

Although Bloom and his colleagues devised a taxonomy of affective objectives, it is not widely used in higher education. A more practical system, based on values clarification research (Raths, Harmin, and Simon, 1966), is presented in modified form in this guide. It envisions three levels of commitment to professional (or other) values:

- Choosing the targeted value freely from among examined alternatives
- Affirming the value publicly
- Acting consistently and repeatedly in accordance with the value

This model is illustrated in detail in Section 9.4, Measures of Professional Orientation.

The performance-oriented outcomes identified by the AECC — intellectual, interpersonal and communication skills, and professional orientation — are among the most important in current educational reform, yet the most challenging to assess. The chapters on measurement that follow describe practical approaches to assessment of these outcomes.

FIGURE 6.2
BLOOM'S TAXONOMY: COGNITIVE DOMAIN[2]

Knowledge: Recall or recognize information (terminology, facts, conventions, trends, sequences, classification systems, categories, criteria, methods, principles or generalizations, theories).
Key words: Define, list, identify, distinguish, summarize, paraphrase.
Example: Student will be able to define terms such as investments, portfolio, equity, debt securities, ROR, ROI, LCM, equity method, market value method with generally accepted account principles (GAAP).

Comprehension: Restate concepts or procedures through translation, interpretation, or extrapolation.
Key words: Explain in own words, describe, translate, illustrate, draw, demonstrate, reorder, differentiate, rephrase.
Example: Student will be able to explain the portfolio approach outlined by GAAP.

Application: Use knowledge to achieve a specific purpose; some discretion or inventiveness may be required.
Key words: Apply, generalize, relate, organize, employ, transfer, restructure, classify.
Example: Student will be able to apply the fair value method for short-term debt and equity investments or equity method for long-term investments to develop a portfolio worksheet.

Analysis: Extract essential elements, relationships, or principles of a problem, situation, theory, idea, etc.
Key words: Compare, contrast, relate, detect, classify, discriminate, deduce, distinguish, quantify, analyze statistically.
Example: Student will be able to analyze risk, liquidity, and ROR on total investment portfolio.

Synthesis: Combine and integrate ideas and information from a variety of sources to create an original product (communication, plan, abstract relationship).
Key words: Design, predict, produce, construct, write, tell, originate, modify, document, formulate, combine, extrapolate, develop, invent, relate.
Example: Student will be able to design a plan to determine consistency between goal for and performance of investment portfolio.

Evaluation: Identify the most desirable choice or action in a choice situation in terms of internal evidence or external criteria.
Key words: Evaluate, test, judge, validate, access, decide, determine, argue, consider, appraise, recommend.
Example: Student will be able to prepare a report providing advice on future investment decisions based on information derived from the analysis and plan (above).

---

[2]Adapted from Bloom, 1956; Mefessel and others, 1967.

CHAPTER 7

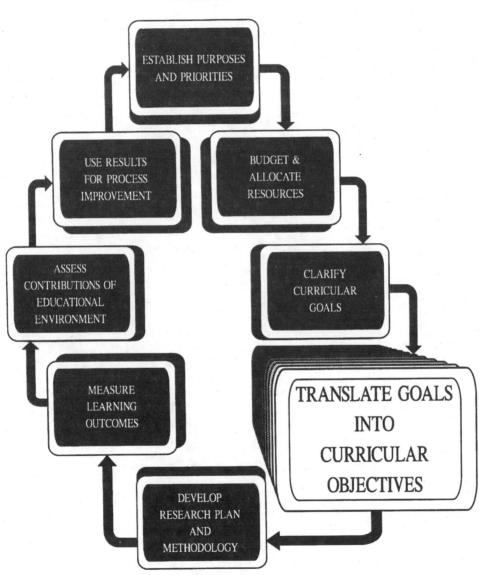

Chapter 7
TRANSLATING GOALS INTO CURRICULAR OBJECTIVES

This chapter continues the work of Chapter 6. It outlines the process by which curricular goals are translated into objectives (or performance outcomes) as a prelude to development of measures for judging students' achievements. This chapter:

- Describes how learning outcomes can be operationally defined, that is, specified in a form that facilitates measurement
- Identifies pitfalls in writing objectives or performance outcomes
- Discusses the transition from objectives to measurement

7.1 Operationally Defining Program Goals

Objectives are operationally defined statements of desired learning outcomes, that is, they are stated in a form that allows measurement. *Goals* such as acquiring "knowledge," "understanding," or "appreciation" provide general direction to faculty in developing instruction but may leave students uncertain about how to approach course material. In contrast, *objectives* specify the required performance to increase clarity about expectations.

Using the taxonomy introduced in Chapter 6, the department can construct objectives representing a continuum of levels of understanding that can serve as milestones marking students' progress through the program.

Well-defined objectives greatly simplify the selection and design of methods for measuring learning outcomes. Objectives should answer the following questions:

- *Content:* What do students need to *know* about this subject?
- *Action:* How do we want students to *use* that knowledge?
- *Context:* Under what *circumstances* will students be expected to demonstrate their knowledge?
- *Performance Criteria:* What are the *standards* that will be used to judge students' performance?

The following examples illustrate two applications of this schema:

Example 1: Working collaboratively with a team of peers (context), graduating seniors will be able to identify and solve unstructured, real-world problems (action) related to audit situations (content). The result should include an analysis of the problem, at least two plausible alternative solutions, and a convincing rationale stating why the final solution proposal is preferred (performance criteria).

Example 2: Upon completing the internship program (context), graduating seniors will be able to identify and solve unstructured real-world problems (action) drawn from professional practice in taxation (content) to the satisfaction of trained raters [faculty, employers, internship supervisors] (performance standard).

Content: Both examples identify the general domain in which students are expected to demonstrate their knowledge.

Action: Both examples specify actions students must take to demonstrate achievement of the goal. The actions identified for these intellectual skills correspond to high-level objectives in Bloom's cognitive taxonomy.

Context: Each example specifies the context or conditions under which the desired action is expected to be performed. A variety of contexts can be specified, for example, a formal examination (no books, no notes), an actual practice situation, or a simulation.

Performance Criteria: The first example specifies three criteria for judging the students' performance: problem analysis, two alternative solutions, and convincing rationale. These criteria provide a framework for measurement across a variety of tasks. The second example does not specify performance criteria, but refers to rater training, a procedure in which judges agree on the use of criteria tailored to the performance situation. Procedures for training raters are described in Chapter 9.

Performance criteria can be generated through:

- Brainstorming
- Discussing students' work to identify features that distinguish between exemplary and unsatisfactory work
- Analyzing the performance of successful practicing professionals (Greenberg and Smith, 1991)
- Reviewing literature to identify features of successful performance supported by research

Performance criteria developed for program-level assessment can be used by faculty to prepare checklists, rating forms, questionnaires, tests, and other materials for instruction and evaluation (see Chapter 9). Course-embedded assessments tailored to departmental criteria can be compiled in student portfolios and rated using instruments based on the criteria. Scores can then be consolidated to develop a diagnostic profile of students' strengths and weaknesses. In addition, feedback from faculty members who attempt to apply the performance criteria in their courses is a valuable source of information for review and revision of the criteria.

7.2 Pitfalls in Defining Objectives

When formulating objectives, several pitfalls can be avoided. The following are most commonly encountered:

- Writing objectives and performance criteria without reference to students' work
- Over-emphasizing low-level objectives
- Specifying the instructional activity rather than the learning outcome
- Writing outcome statements that are too vague to be measurable

Writing objectives and performance criteria without reference to course syllabi and students' work: Objectives written without reference to what students actually accomplish may prove confusing or irrelevant when faculty attempt to apply them to performance.

Faculty who turn to course syllabi, assignments, and examples of student coursework will find they are better able to articulate what they expect of students.

Developing objectives and performance criteria is not linear nor sequential, but rather iterative and evolutionary. The evolution of specific objectives for a particular goal (such as understanding international accounting) might include the following phases:

- Review relevant course materials and student work
- Draft a statement of objective(s) and criteria
- Use the criteria to review additional examples from the same pool
- Revise objectives and criteria until consensus is reached

Articulating what the faculty *really* want from students is a challenging but crucial step in developing a well-integrated curriculum and corresponding assessment program.

Over-emphasizing low-level objectives: A common pitfall when writing cognitive objectives is to focus primarily on outcomes at low levels of Bloom's taxonomy (knowledge and comprehension) or that require only basic application of concepts. Such objectives require students to do little more than memorize coursework without having to apply or extrapolate that knowledge, or use it to make judgments about complex situations.

When specifying cognitive outcomes, it is important to include the full range of cognitive abilities. The key words presented in Figure 6.2 can be used as a guide when writing objectives at higher levels of Bloom's taxonomy.

Specifying the instructional activity rather than the learning outcome: Objectives are frequently written to identify what the student or faculty member will *do* rather than how the student will be able to put that knowledge to use. For example, the statement, "Students will learn the basic principles of financial accounting" describes the instructor's *intent* but does not state what students will be able to *do* once they have "learned" basic principles. The statement, "The instructor will present guidelines for design of advanced information systems" describes what the *teacher* will do but neglects to specify the intended result of students' capabilities with respect to advanced information systems. In contrast an outcome statement would read, "Students will be able to apply guidelines to the design of advanced information systems."

Writing outcome statements that are too vague to be measurable: A fourth pitfall is to write objectives that are not stated in measurable form. For example, the AECC *Objectives* lists "Taxation and its impact on financial and managerial decisions" as an important program goal under "Accounting Knowledge." Interpreted as a goal ("Students will demonstrate knowledge of taxation...") this general statement provides little guidance for measurement; however, it can be used to generate a variety of objectives. For example:

- Students will be able to *explain* the key provisions and exceptions in the tax code (knowledge level)
- Students will be able to *justify* financial and managerial decisions incorporating taxation principles (evaluation level)

The addition of an action-oriented verb (italicized) clarifies *how* students will demonstrate their knowledge.

Similarly, accounting knowledge related to "the nature of attest services and the conceptual and procedural bases for performing them" (*Objectives*, p. 8) can be interpreted in any of the following ways:

- Students will be able to *list* and briefly *summarize* principle characteristics of the attest function (knowledge level)
- Students will be able to *explain* the importance of the attest function and describe the conceptual and procedural bases for performing it (comprehension level)
- Students will be able to *conduct* a simulated audit using correct procedures for the attest function (synthesis level)

For clarity of instruction and assessment, faculty should specify the level or levels desired.

7.3 The Transition from Objectives to Measurement

Objectives need not be written to conform exactly to a single standard. However, objectives stated in terms of *actions to be performed by students* operationally define the desired outcomes so that measurement indicators can more readily be identified. The objectives should be precise enough to suggest measurement strategies, yet broad enough to encompass a wide range of teaching approaches. Clarity and consensus about the goals, objectives and performance may evolve slowly or emerge quickly, depending on the maturity of the program and the degree of consensus among faculty about its purposes.

In a dynamic, responsive program environment, goals and objectives will be refined periodically as faculty understanding of learning outcomes and graduates' professional needs increase. The most important feature of effective outcome statements is the integration of the mission of the program and the institution, the values and instructional aims of the faculty, the characteristics of the students, and the needs of the profession.

CHAPTER 8

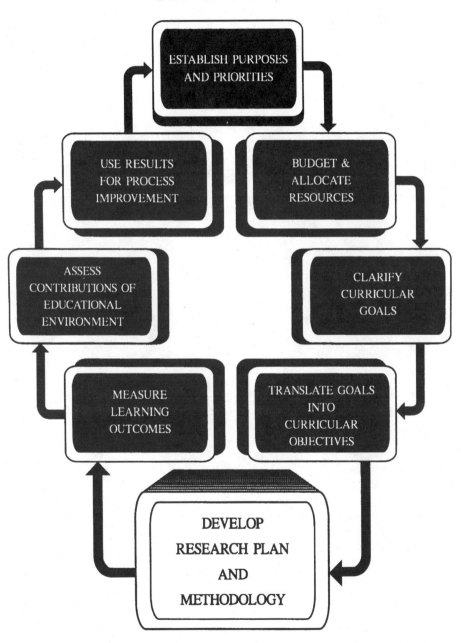

ESTABLISH PURPOSES
AND PRIORITIES

USE RESULTS
FOR PROCESS
IMPROVEMENT

BUDGET &
ALLOCATE
RESOURCES

ASSESS
CONTRIBUTIONS OF
EDUCATIONAL
ENVIRONMENT

CLARIFY
CURRICULAR
GOALS

MEASURE
LEARNING
OUTCOMES

TRANSLATE GOALS
INTO
CURRICULAR
OBJECTIVES

DEVELOP
RESEARCH PLAN
AND
METHODOLOGY

Chapter 8
DEVELOPING THE RESEARCH PLAN
AND METHODOLOGY

The assessment research plan translates the purpose of assessment (Chapter 4) into a method or methods of inquiry to fulfill that purpose. The assessment committee determines the nature and scope of the inquiry, then selects appropriate research methods, analytical techniques, variables to be included, measures needed, subgroups to be studied, and sample sizes.

This chapter outlines options and offers suggestions for determining what is necessary, sufficient, and feasible within the resources of the department. It is intended to clarify the role of traditional research design in assessment, and to suggest research approaches and issues especially relevant in the accounting context. Chapter 9 follows with guidelines for selecting and/or developing measurement instruments. Specifically, this chapter:

- Identifies criteria for selecting research designs and methods
- Outlines basic paradigms for educational assessment
- Identifies design issues especially relevant to educational assessment
- Suggests designs that allow the assessment program to develop gradually
- Offers practical, credible ways to obtain data for assessment
- Notes ethical issues related to educational research

8.1 Criteria for Selecting the Research Approach

A department contemplating an assessment initiative can set its sights on publication-quality research, on informal studies for internal use, or on a degree of sophistication intermediate between these two extremes. A primary concern in assessment is whether the benefits will justify the costs involved.

Most fundamentally, the design should yield results that serve the purposes identified for assessment, which in turn should be formulated to respond to the information needs of key stakeholders (as described in Chapter 4). The scope and formality of the inquiry depend on the purposes of the assessment, who will use the results, and what is at stake. This section proposes five criteria for selection of research methods tailored to departmental needs.

Four criteria proposed by the Joint Committee on Standards for Educational Evaluation (1981) offer a starting point:

- *Relevance to Policy Decisions and Planning:* The methodology chosen should yield results that will help to answer the policy or planning questions that prompted the study in the first place.
- *Feasibility:* The scope of the plan should fall well within the resources and time available.
- *Credibility:* The technical quality of the study should be sufficient to allow reasonable certainty in drawing conclusions based on the results obtained.

- *Propriety:* The approach should conform to legal and ethical standards for the conduct of research on human subjects (adapted from Davis, 1989, p. 18).

Assessment differs from traditional educational evaluation in one important respect: it should be designed to *assist the learner.* This aspect of the design affects both student and faculty willingness to participate. The assessment design should therefore respond to an important additional criterion:

- *Benefit to Participants:* The approach should provide some immediate benefit for all those who participate, but especially the students and faculty most directly involved.

Together, these criteria suggest a flexible approach to assessment research design. For example, the "credibility" criterion suggests that good design is important, but the "feasibility" criterion will often preclude obtaining publication-quality data. The sampling plan and methods should nonetheless meet credibility standards of the department for internal use, since the results may influence allocation of resources.

Credibility is enhanced by "triangulation," that is, the use of data from several sources to enhance interpretation of data from any one source and to strengthen the plausibility of inferences from all sources. Triangulation cannot overcome all the weaknesses of non-experimental designs, nor can it compensate for poorly designed instruments. However, triangulation does help faculty to interpret data by providing more than one perspective on the question at hand.

The assessment committee can facilitate integration of the criteria by recommending approaches that incorporate assessment measures within the normal requirements of instruction. Referred to as "course-embedded" assessment, this strategy offers a practical way to obtain data within a variety of research designs. Because it makes assessment an integral part of teaching, course-embedded assessment facilitates faculty participation and interest (Ewell, 1991b). It also benefits participating students since they receive instructor feedback on the work they produce for assessment. Evaluating students' work on clearly identified performance criteria also benefits them by promoting the important lifelong learning skill of self-assessment. These benefits are increased when the professor introduces the performance criteria and discusses their application to students' work (Loacker and others, 1984; Loacker, Cromwell, and O'Brien, 1986).

When seeking a research approach that responds to the five criteria, the assessment committee should consider lessons learned by the organizers of the Harvard Assessment Seminar:

An incorrect expectation was that larger-scale, elaborate studies would be especially interesting to most participants [in the Seminar]. We misjudged this badly, and now believe that less can be more. Sometimes a small effort with a quick turnaround, if well done, is the most effective research of all. This is especially true when the findings from a project may affect a policy decision and the person in charge of policy has specially requested research to help shape the decision (Light and others, 1990, p. 236).

8.2 Research Options for Educational Assessment

Two modes of inquiry contribute to a balanced and informative assessment portfolio:

- *Concurrent* inquiry to monitor and respond to program outcomes and client satisfaction *during* implementation
- *Retrospective* inquiry to determine program effectiveness and identify contributing factors, generally upon completion of a program cycle

Concurrent inquiry is similar to "formative" evaluation (that is, contributing to the development and improvement of the program). *Retrospective* inquiry is similar to "summative" evaluation (providing data to judge the merits of the program) because it is implemented at the end of a program cycle. However, retrospective inquiry should contribute to continuing improvement of the program in future cycles. The appropriate balance between concurrent and retrospective inquiry depends on the purposes and audiences for the assessment.

Within these two modes of inquiry, research design options for educational assessment fall into four general paradigms: descriptive, relational, experimental, and quasi-experimental studies (adapted from Light, Singer, and Willett, 1990; see also Williams and others, 1988):

- *Descriptive* research designs examine student characteristics, the educational environment, or learning outcomes separately and at a single point in time. Descriptive studies may use either qualitative or quantitative methods, or a combination of the two.

Descriptive studies answer questions such as, "What are our graduates' strengths and weaknesses with respect to a particular learning outcome?" or "What skills related to use of information technology do our students have on entry to the program?"

- *Relational* studies examine the degree of association between student characteristics, the educational environment, and/or learning outcomes. Relational models include cross-sectional, simple correlational, and multivariate designs (ANCOVA, multiple regression, causal modeling).

Relational studies answer questions such as, "What subgroup(s) of students would be excluded from the program if we required demonstrated competency in writing?" or "What are the differential effects of an innovative program for students with different characteristics?"

- *Experimental* studies use random assignment to experimental and control groups to establish *causal* links between the educational environment (independent variables) and learning outcomes (dependent variables). The most common design is the "pretest-posttest control group design"; however, the "posttest-only control group design" is equally valid if students have been randomly assigned to groups (Campbell and Stanley, 1966).
- *Quasi-experimental* designs are often necessary in educational settings, where it is difficult to assign students randomly to groups. Quasi-experimental designs reduce threats to validity and reliability, for example, by using repeated measurement with an experimental condition introduced at one or more points of measurement (the "time series" design; Campbell and Stanley, 1966) or by including student characteristics as covariates in the analysis to reduce the effects of self-selection bias (Light and others, 1990).

Experimental and quasi-experimental studies answer questions such as, "Which of three instructional methods has the greatest impact on professionally-related writing skills of students in upper-division accounting courses?"

Descriptive designs are most often associated with concurrent (formative) inquiry. Retrospective inquiries employ the full range of design paradigms, but especially the correlational and experimental or quasi-experimental methods.

8.3 Design Issues in the Assessment of Learning Outcomes

Familiarity with research design principles and statistical methods is an important asset brought by accounting faculty to the task of assessment. Accounting faculty may be less familiar, however, with design issues associated with studies of learning outcomes. This section identifies several such issues.

Issue 1: Interactions between student characteristics and the educational environment: Educational research designs frequently take into account the interaction between student characteristics and the educational environment. Researchers today are less likely to ask, "Which method is best?" and more likely to ask, "Which method is best for whom?" (Snow and Peterson, 1980, p. 2). For example, students who transfer into accounting are more interested in expanded learning outcomes (such as those advocated by the AECC) than those who began their college careers as accounting majors (Inman, Wenzler, and Wickert, 1989). A study of students' responses to an innovative junior-year program might therefore take into account both transfer status and initial interest in the expanded outcomes.

Many student characteristics can affect the outcomes achieved by a program. For example, prior knowledge (both general and task-specific) is a good predictor of students' performance on learning tasks. This well-established relationship underlies the use of measures such as admission test scores and GPA as covariates in studies of college outcomes (see for example, Astin, 1993; Pascarella and Terenzini, 1991). Similarly, prior interest in the subject is an important predictor of satisfaction (Marsh, 1980). Accordingly, self-reported motivation to take the course is used as a control variable in a widely-used nationally-normed instrument for assessing students' responses to instruction (Center for Faculty Evaluation and Development, 1975).

Less familiar to many faculty but important in fostering lifelong learning are characteristics such as students' preferred strategies for learning and their motivational orientation. For example, students who are motivated to learn independently benefit more from innovative learning experiences than those motivated to learn by conforming (Domino, 1971). In one study, assigning students to a section designed for their motivational orientation would have increased the scores of 44% of the sample by 12 to 25 percentile points. An additional 10% of the students would have improved by as much as 40 percentile points (Peterson, 1979).

Learning styles also influence students' ability to benefit from different educational environments. For example, "Sensors," who process information in terms of concrete details, prefer an emphasis on factual information and standardized procedures. "Intuitives," who process information in terms of connections and possibilities, prefer learning environments that encourage them to develop their own ideas (using the Myers-Briggs Type Inventory; Schroeder, 1993). In a recent study comparing CAI and lecture methods in elementary accounting, Sensors performed better with lecture instruction than CAI, while the reverse was true for Intuitive students (Ott, Mann, and Moores, 1990). Most accounting students prefer the Sensing mode (Geary and Rooney, 1993).

Including student characteristics in the research design improves the chances that program effects on learning outcomes will be detected rather than averaged out. More importantly, use of student characteristics in designing instruction may increase overall student success in the program. At the same time, students should be challenged to expand their repertoire of learning strategies for greater professional adaptability.

Issue 2: The Trend Toward "Naturalistic" Modes of Inquiry: To date, few departments have undertaken formal experimental studies of curricular innovations and outcomes. Among the AECC grant institutions, the University of North Texas (Bayer and others, 1993) and Arizona State University (McKenzie, 1991) were noteworthy for their use of experimental designs with pre- and posttesting and comparison groups.

Discussing the feasibility of a traditional control-group design, BYU faculty involved in the AECC-funded junior year core program comment:

> Desirable as it may seem at first glance, this type of design would break down were it invoked in evaluating the junior core program. Since the technical competencies in the new program are somewhat different from those in the traditional program, there is no way to obtain a comparable control group. Further, we could not simply administer a pre-test at the beginning of the year and a post-test at the end. Without a control group, there is no way to attribute any change to the program. Finally, even if a suitable control group could be found and the new group showed greater gains, we would have no way of deciding what aspect of the program made the difference. Too many variables are at work in a new program, not the least of which is the Hawthorne effect (BYU Vol. I, 1992, p. 61).

The desire to benefit students and increase feasibility has led faculty to adopt classroom-centered, naturalistic assessment strategies such as capstone experiences, portfolios, and use of faculty-designed, course-embedded instruments rather than standardized achievement tests. A trend toward the use of naturalistic approaches is increasingly evident in surveys of current assessment practice (Ewell, 1991b). The assessment methodologies used by BYU faculty, described in Section 8.4, illustrate this trend.

Issue 3: Design for results with practical significance: Research that is not directly useful in program planning, or that yields minimal results, may lead faculty to question the value of the assessment program, or to conclude that little can be done to improve students' skills. Yet the underlying problem may be that the intervention was not broad enough in scope to yield a visible result.

Effecting meaningful change in learning outcomes may require a far greater degree of change in the program than faculty expect. Curricular changes such as reorganizing topics or adding modules or even courses may have limited impact on learning outcomes. For example, ethics instruction in a single course rarely produces significant gains on measures of ethical reasoning (Conry and Nelson, 1989; Ponemon, 1993). Critical thinking is similarly resistant to brief instructional interventions (Kurfiss, 1988; McMillan, 1987). Increasing writing *assignments* without a corresponding increase in writing *instruction* may have only limited impact on measures of writing skill. Achieving results of practical significance may require both a change of curricular emphasis and a qualitative change in the *way* students are taught.

Early results from the University of Southern California's Year 2000 Curriculum Project suggest the degree of change necessary to achieve attention-getting results. Early indicators of this program's impact include:

- Increased number of applications for admission to the accounting program
- Increased enrollment in the program
- Reduced drop rates (down to 3% with *tougher* grading standards)
- More diverse students (attracted from other majors, for example, political science students drawn initially by the course's inclusion of government examples)

Faculty have informally noted increases in students' "intellectual aggressiveness," "teamwork and communication skills," and "awareness of business issues" (Pincus, in press). These impressions of important learning outcomes could be verified, for example, by examining student portfolios and by surveying employers of alumni.

It would be impossible to isolate a single cause of these changes. The course has been modified in at least the following ways:

- A focus on the user, not the preparer, and on concepts and tools rather than rules
- An integrated approach to accounting education, introducing basic concepts and issues across all the functional areas of accounting — including systems, tax, auditing, financial and management accounting
- An accent on contemporary examples and current events involving international and domestic business, non-profit and government organizations
- An emphasis on skill development, as well as technical accounting knowledge— including group assignments, written and oral presentation assignments, electronic research assignments, and assignments concerned with ethics and values
- Course and instructor materials that support a change to an interactive learning environment (excerpted from Pincus, in press)

Virtually any feasible design will leave unanswered important questions about "what works" in such a complex program. Still, the USC program advances discussion of curricular and pedagogical innovation by demonstrating that a dramatic departure from normal practice can indeed have an immediate impact on students' success in and response to the course.

8.4 Design Options for Gradual Evolution of the Assessment Program

The designs chosen in the early stages of assessment should permit gradual evolution of the assessment program. Some suggestions follow.

Descriptive studies: Descriptive studies can yield immediate program information and can also serve as a baseline for future longitudinal comparisons. Many institutions conduct annual surveys of students and graduates that include self-reported gains on a variety of learning outcomes along with measures of client satisfaction. Including such questions, along with identification of the student by major, is an inexpensive way to obtain student feedback on the program. The results will usually suggest areas for further study.

Course-embedded measures can be combined to obtain a profile of students' accomplishments over time using the "portfolio assessment" method. The professor assigns projects related to targeted objectives and provides prompt feedback to individual students using performance criteria for that objective. Students compile their work into portfolios for subsequent review by a faculty subcommittee. The subcommittee reviews a selected sample of portfolios in a program-level study of students' strengths and weaknesses on the targeted objectives.

In accounting, the portfolio could include one or more case studies, an edited paper, a significant individual research project, and a cooperative group project. Or a single, major case study can be used to assess several skills such as writing, complex problem solving, and ethical reasoning (a high-stakes assessment unless used in concert with other measures). Students' work in two or three courses can be included in the portfolio to allow assessment of skills across a range of content areas.

The credibility of findings from the portfolio approach is enhanced by building "interrater reliability" among those who will judge the portfolios (Chapter 9) and using a systematic sampling procedure to select assignments or portfolios for review. Systematic sampling, rather than attempting to review all portfolios, also enhances feasibility.

When using the portfolio review model, faculty may question student ownership of the work submitted. One solution is to include samples of work completed both during and outside of class (Belanoff and Elbow, 1986). An example in accounting would be an in-class essay demonstrating the ability to interpret financial data or spontaneously analyze a complex accounting situation.

Building on Descriptive Foundations: In the descriptive study outlined above, the first set of portfolios reveal students' current capabilities, whether sophomores, juniors, or seniors. Later, the assessment committee can add data for other student groups, and continue to collect data over a period of years. This strategy eventually allows for analysis of developmental change in individual students and trends in program outcomes across cohorts. The initial descriptive study therefore evolves into a relational study. If innovations are introduced, their impact can be assessed using the quasi-experimental time series design (Campbell and Stanley, 1966).

Validation Studies: Another option is to validate an instrument designed to measure students' progress on a high-priority outcome of the program. Performance assessments in particular warrant validation. For example, the assessment committee could recommend a study to determine whether a performance measure used to predict graduates' professional success adds value (such as unique diagnostic insight) compared to more readily accessible measures such as faculty ratings. A different type of validation study would be necessary to determine whether a measure is biased toward or against a particular group of students, for example women or international students. (For additional suggestions see Light and others, 1990.) Validation studies can result in a useful contribution to the profession as well as to departmental understanding of its assessment measures.

Immediate feedback studies for monitoring instructional innovations: When the faculty implement major changes in curriculum and/or instruction, concurrent inquiry with quick turnaround time can be essential to strengthen the program and prevent major problems from developing.

BYU's "ethnographic" approach satisfied the faculty's need for quick turnaround of data. The faculty wanted to monitor their new curriculum while it was being implemented so that they could make mid-program adjustments if necessary. They included a variety of qualitative, concurrent inquiry methods in their design:

- Regular sack-lunch discussions with students about the program
- Videotapes and observations of actual class sessions
- Exchange and study of faculty teaching plans
- Descriptions of office hour visits
- Examination of samples of student work
- Frequent meetings and retreats to discuss the program

The BYU faculty supplemented this qualitative approach with a traditional exit examination to assess learning outcomes. Their approach illustrates a mix of concurrent and retrospective, formal and informal assessment strategies. Assessment became an integral part of program planning and improvement.

Relational studies: Today, relational studies frequently use multivariate analytical techniques to identify the relative weight of factors contributing to a specified learning outcome. Such studies can provide valuable insight regarding the role of student characteristics and features of the educational environment in achievement of a particular outcome. Data for these studies can be stored on a departmental database. Building and gradually enhancing the database gives accounting faculty a flexible, familiar tool for tracking students, monitoring program outcomes, and exploring questions about the program's impact on students.

A recent study illustrates the value of using relational methodology and data from multiple institutions. Data were obtained from three institutions with varying proportions of minority students (primarily African American). The researchers used regression and analysis of variance to determine the predictive power of high school grade-point average (HSGPA) and students' expected grades for minority and "majority" students (male and female), using withdrawal after the third week and course grades as the dependent variables (Carpenter, Friar, and Lipe, 1993).

The researchers found that minority males were most likely to withdraw. For these students (unlike majority students), withdrawing from the course was unrelated to HSGPA but strongly related to expected grades; actual grades, however, were less strongly related to expectations for minority students when compared to majority students. These findings suggest that efforts to retain African American students might begin by helping them develop realistic expectations, then provide academic support to increase their chances of success.

Experimental and quasi-experimental studies: Results from descriptive and relational studies often suggest hypotheses about program changes that will improve learning outcomes. The study just described, for instance, might lead faculty to propose a program to address the expectations brought to the institution by students of color. Small-scale pilot studies using experimental methods are useful for testing the effectiveness of such innovations. Other changes that lend themselves to experimental study include new applications of technology or an enhanced writing or speaking component. As noted in Section 8.4, inclusion of student characteristics adds depth to the study and increases the chances of a meaningful result (for example, see Ott and others, 1990).

Research conducted for purposes of educational assessment will rarely satisfy traditional criteria for research quality. Nonetheless, well-planned pilot studies, descriptive and relational studies, and highly focused experimental and quasi-experimental designs can provide timely and relevant information that is significantly more reliable and valid than anecdotal evidence and impressionistic reports.

8.5 Practical Ways to Obtain Data for Assessment

Often the most perplexing challenge in educational assessment is how to obtain a reasonably representative or complete sample of students. The use of course-embedded measures is one important response to this challenge, one of few strategies ideally suited to assessment of learning outcomes. Other potentially useful data collection strategies are suggested below:

- Use electronic mail networks and bulletin boards to surface students' questions, understanding of the subject, and/or responses to instruction while the course or innovation is in progress.
- Regularly distribute brief, anonymous program questionnaires through the faculty. Use a simple "report card" format. Or pose questions focused on outcomes ("What is the most important concept you have learned in this course so far?") or on the educational environment ("What one thing would you change about the program if you could? What aspect of the program most helps you learn?"). Ask faculty to allocate 5-10 minutes of class time to the questionnaires every 3-4 weeks. Faculty can scan results for their students and make brief reports at a department meeting.
- Set up sack lunch meetings to discuss the program.
- Have teams of students make 20-minute presentations at a series of faculty-student luncheon "by invitation only." Make it an honor to participate. Encourage attention to expanded learning outcomes such as creativity, teamwork, group interaction, and relevance. Videotape the presentations to assemble a panorama of student performances. Let the audience provide brief written feedback.
- Set up focus groups in which students must respond to a current issue in accounting. List concepts and resources used by the group, identify approaches they take to the problem, and note how they interact with each other.
- Include self-reports of progress on key learning outcomes as part of the petition to graduate or an automated registration system.

Faculty, students, instructional resource personnel, and practicing professionals can suggest additional methods.

8.6 Ethical Standards for Research with Human Subjects

The American Psychological Association has established ethical standards for research with human subjects. Issues that are often salient in educational research are the right to privacy, voluntary participation, and the right to expect benefits of participation that outweigh the risks (Joint Committee, 1981, as cited in Davis, 1989). Especially relevant to relational and longitudinal studies such as those described above is the need to obtain permission from students prior to accessing their records.

Research involving students is subject to institutional review procedures for the use of human subjects. Educational studies are often considered exempt from formal review, but should be disclosed to the appropriate institutional review body. Most institutions have a policy on the use of human subjects and may also have a human subjects review committee. Because these policies and procedures are required for Federal funding of grants and contracts, information can usually be obtained from the institutional office that administers externally sponsored projects.

CHAPTER 9

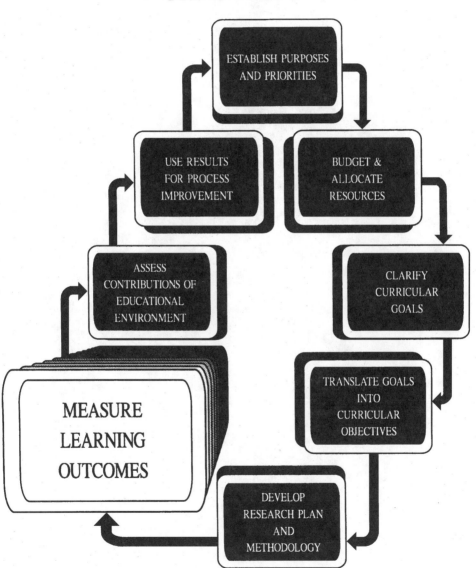

ESTABLISH PURPOSES
AND PRIORITIES

USE RESULTS
FOR PROCESS
IMPROVEMENT

BUDGET &
ALLOCATE
RESOURCES

ASSESS
CONTRIBUTIONS OF
EDUCATIONAL
ENVIRONMENT

CLARIFY
CURRICULAR
GOALS

MEASURE
LEARNING
OUTCOMES

TRANSLATE GOALS
INTO
CURRICULAR
OBJECTIVES

DEVELOP
RESEARCH PLAN
AND
METHODOLOGY

Chapter 9
MEASURING LEARNING OUTCOMES

This chapter describes the development of measures to assess the learning outcomes of the curriculum. Specifically the chapter:

- Identifies criteria for measuring program-level outcomes
- Describes procedures for the design and validation of learning outcome measures
- Describes and illustrates methods for assessing expanded learning outcomes in three categories identified by advocates of change in accounting education:
  - Knowledge (including the ability to adapt and apply knowledge in new ways)
  - Skills (intellectual, interpersonal, communication, and ethical reasoning)
  - Professional orientation (values and attitudes)

A fundamental premise of the *Objectives* is that "To attain and maintain the status of a professional accountant requires continual learning" (p. 1). The curriculum should help students learn how to learn, building on three major components: knowledge, skills, and professional orientation. Assessment of each of these categories is discussed separately in the sections that follow. In addition, assessment of "learning to learn" is discussed with attention to both the skills and attitudes believed to play a part in fostering lifelong learning.

In preparing to examine learning outcomes at the program level, it is useful to keep in mind some key differences between 'classroom-level' and 'program-level' measures of learning outcomes. In the classroom, many measures of *different* outcomes are used to make global judgments about the achievements and relative ranking of *individual* students within a subject area. At the program level, one or more measures of a *single* outcome or family of outcomes may be used to make judgments about the success of the *program*. Measures used for program-level assessment are likely to be developed collaboratively and systematically by teams of faculty rather than by individuals.

A further difference is that program measures are expected to demonstrate degrees of reliability and validity not usually associated with classroom measures. Both classroom- and program-level measurement should, however, be held to rigorous standards because important decisions depend on the results they yield.

Finally, new expectations arising from changes in the accounting profession suggest that program-level assessments will increasingly emphasize *use* of knowledge and skills of learning to learn, a trend which will, in turn, affect assessment at the classroom level.

In spite of their differences, classroom- and program-level measurement should be coherently related and in some cases even intertwined as in the case of portfolio assessment or other course-embedded approaches. Measurement at both levels should address the goals, objectives, and performance criteria established by the faculty (as described in Chapters 6 and 7). These essential outcomes, which shape and direct the curriculum and the design of outcome measures, should be rooted in the instructional materials used by faculty (syllabi, examinations, projects, cases, problems). Some program-level measures may therefore be derived from materials faculty use in their courses. Conversely, development of outcome measures may lead faculty to clarify and refine the goals and objectives, with corresponding changes in instructional materials, methods, or even curricular structure.

Commonly used methods for assessing knowledge and skills (cognitive outcomes) and attitudes and values (affective outcomes) are listed in Figure 9.1.

FIGURE 9.1

Assessing Knowledge and Skills

- Tests and examinations:
  - Scores on in-class examinations
  - Standardized or locally developed achievement tests
  - Oral examinations
- Course grades
- Grade-point averages
- Faculty ratings
- Student self-reports
- Learning logs (question/connect/apply)
- Performance measures and simulations
- Portfolios (collected work of students over time)
- Internship supervisor/employer evaluations
- Assessment center method

Assessing Values and Attitudes

- Questionnaires and rating scales
- Observation/reflection logs
- Focus groups
- Unobtrusive measures (for example, participation rates, choice behavior)
- Performance simulations
- Research instruments

9.1 Basic Principles and Procedures for Designing Learning Outcome Measures

Section 9.1 presents criteria and basic procedures for design and validation of program-level measures. Sections 9.2 through 9.4 offer specific guidance for measurement related to each of the three major categories of learning outcomes. Section 9.5 addresses assessment related to learning to learn.

9.1.1 Criteria for Program-Level Measures

To make program-level judgments with assurance, learning outcome measures should meet several criteria:

- Measures *must* be targeted to specific program goals
- Measures should yield diagnostic feedback about the accounting *program* by revealing patterns of strength and weakness in the performance of a group or groups of students
- Reliability of measurement should be confirmed using methods such as internal consistency checks (useful for multi-item instruments measuring a single construct) and rater agreement checks ("interrater reliability," important when judging complex products or performances)
- Measures should be validated, for example through comparison of results for the same objective using different modes of assessment (e.g., paper-and-pencil analytical tests of problem-solving skill and ratings of performance in simulated or actual problem situations) or by obtaining judgments from practicing professionals for comparison with judgments made by faculty

Initially, not all measures will meet all criteria. Over a period of years, the faculty's understanding of measurement will increase, leading to improvements in the assessment portfolio.

9.1.2 Design Process for Learning Outcome Measures

The procedure for developing measures of learning outcomes is as follows:

- Review targeted *objectives* and *performance criteria* (described in Chapter 7) and clarify if necessary
- Select or devise *measurement instruments* and *rating criteria* that *best* represent achievement of the desired performance
- Obtain *performance data* from students
- Apply rating criteria to obtain *performance ratings or judgments*
- Determine *reliability* and *validity* of measures
- *Recalibrate measurement:* review instruments and/or procedures periodically and make needed improvements

Application of this basic procedure will be described for each major category of learning outcomes.

It is not necessary to develop separate measures for each goal or objective. Instead, areas of legitimate overlap should be identified to simplify assessment and reduce costs. For example, a complex, realistic case (such as the multi-media program *Dermaceutics, Inc.*, produced by Coopers & Lybrand, or the *CableCo Chronicles*) can be used to assess professional knowledge, interpersonal skills, critical thinking and complex problem solving, ethical decision-making and professional orientation. To avoid contamination of ratings ("halo effect"), students' performance in each goal area should be rated separately, preferably by different raters. However, a single performance measure should be supplemented by other measures to strengthen interpretation of results.

9.1.3 Reliability and Validity of Outcome Measures

As already noted, a key difference between measures developed for classroom use and those used for program assessment is that greater care is often exercised in program assessment to demonstrate reliability and validity. These terms apply as follows:

Reliability is the degree to which a test minimizes errors due to problems of measurement. A test with only a few items is not as reliable as a longer one, because with fewer items it is less certain that results are not obtained by chance. A reliable measure will yield consistent results when the same sample is tested repeatedly (assuming no relevant intervention has occurred).

Reliability of multi-item tests is frequently estimated based on the internal consistency of responses, using correlational measures such as the Kuder-Richardson formula. The higher the correlation, the more likely that the test is measuring a single quality or characteristic—in this case, students' knowledge of course content. For program evaluation, reliabilities around .60 are acceptable, although higher reliability is recommended if results will be used to advise or make decisions about individual students (Erwin, 1991; Banta and Schneider, 1988).

For performance rating scales, reliability is the degree to which observers agree when rating the same performance independently. This is referred to as interrater reliability (a concept similar to "objectivity" in the accounting literature; see Section 9.3 for procedures). Interrater reliabilities should reach a minimum of 70% (Erwin, 1991).

Validity is an estimate of the degree to which the instrument measures what it is intended to measure (Erwin, 1991). Two basic forms are *content* validity and *construct* validity.

   - *Content validity:* In the judgment of experts, the content of the test accurately reflects the content of the course or program on which it is based.
   - *Construct validity:* Results obtained from the measure are consistent with other measures associated with the underlying trait or "construct." For example, performance on a formal assessment of oral communication skills in accounting should be positively correlated with grades in courses that require extensive use of public speaking skills and with supervisor or employer ratings of on-the-job communication skills. Scores on an exit test for accounting seniors should predict performance as a practicing accountant (sometimes referred to as "predictive" or "criterion" validity).

Standardized tests such as the CPA exam have been criticized because they do not have high construct (predictive) validity (Ferris, 1982); that is, scores on these tests are not highly correlated with success in the accounting profession. Similarly, ratings of internships may appear to be valid because they reflect actual professional performance. However, if the internship experience includes only routine tasks, it affords little opportunity for the supervisor to judge students' performance on more challenging tasks that may actually better reflect professional practice.

When performance measures are used, only a few situations can usually be assessed, so reliability and predictive validity of results are problematic. Using many performance-oriented assessments (case studies, projects, and internship evaluations) from a variety of sources gives faculty a more complete profile of students' capabilities, strengthening the reliability and validity of resulting judgments.

For further discussion of reliability and validity, see Light and others (1990) and Williams and others (1988).

9.1.4 Norm-Referenced and Criterion-Referenced Testing

Before designing or selecting a test, it is important to know whether results will be used to compare students' performance to that of other students or to determine whether each student has achieved a pre-defined level of performance.

> *Norm-referenced* tests are designed to rank-order students' performances relative to each other. A norm-referenced test should yield a standard distribution of scores, on the assumption that ability is normally distributed in the subject population. The use of standardized norm-referenced tests allows for comparisons between students at different institutions.

> *Criterion-referenced* tests are intended to determine how well students perform relative to the objectives and performance criteria for the course or program. A criterion-referenced test should yield a positively skewed distribution, assuming the test is valid, instruction has been effective, and students have participated actively in the learning process.

The distribution of scores is a joint function of the *difficulty level* of each test item, defined as the percentage of students who respond correctly, and the *item discrimination index*, defined as the degree to which students' performance on each item is consistent with their performance on the overall test (Erwin, 1991; McBeath, 1992). For *norm-referenced* testing, items should be written to yield an average item difficulty of about .5. For *criterion-referenced* tests, item difficulties (percent correct) should be somewhat higher; that is, the majority of students should be able to reach the criterion (usually 80% or 90% correct). If many students fail to reach the criterion, the test, instructional emphasis or methodology, and students' background preparation should be reviewed. Items with moderate difficulties should have a discrimination index of at least .30 (McBeath, 1992).

Test analysis programs can be used to obtain these figures for each item on the test. Such information is useful for validating a test and also for determining whether it should be kept in the item pool, modified, or discarded. For a summary of basic test design and validation procedures, see McBeath (1992).

Generally, program-level measures should be *criterion-referenced* rather than *norm-referenced*, since the purpose is to determine whether the program facilitates students' achievement rather than to compare students' performances to each other. Standardized, norm-referenced instruments are appropriate when comparisons between students at different institutions are desired.

9.1.5 Choosing Standardized or Locally-Developed Instruments

An important decision for the assessment of knowledge outcomes is how much to rely on commercially available standardized examinations and how deeply to get involved in developing measures in-house. Each has advantages and disadvantages, summarized in Figure 9.2. Although the costs are not insignificant, faculty involvement in developing outcome measures offers important benefits, for example, enhanced curricular consistency, improved classroom testing, and greater faculty attention to application of knowledge (Banta and Schneider, 1988, pp. 78-79). Experience further indicates that

...the programs that have invested time and effort in designing their own exams have made the most use of students' scores. These faculties have been more ego-involved in the outcomes of testing, since they made the decision about what content should be tested and by what means (Banta, 1985, p. 27).

Class assignments and examinations should reflect curricular objectives and incorporate basic test development and validation procedures such as those described below.

9.2 Measuring Knowledge Outcomes

It is often tempting to initiate an assessment program by administering a standardized, machine-scored test of knowledge to seniors. This strategy has several limitations:

FIGURE 9.2
COMPARING STANDARDIZED AND LOCALLY DEVELOPED
ACHIEVEMENT EXAMINATIONS

STANDARDIZED EXAMS

Advantages	Disadvantages
• lower opportunity cost to obtain and administer test • high level of technical quality (valid, reliable) • reflect expert views of what students should know • national norms allow comparison of individuals and/or groups or to an absolute standard (criterion) • quick and convenient if available for departmental use	• limited options to choose from • test content may not be consistent with program objectives • test content may lack breadth of content and scope of skills measured • comparative testing communicates competitive ethic • forced-choice testing communicates low priority on creativity • availability may be limited to public testing sessions • low student motivation to take test if no personal consequences or intrinsic value

LOCALLY DEVELOPED EXAMS

Advantages	Disadvantages
• can be designed to match program objectives • scope and length of test can be adjusted to departmental needs • faculty involvement fosters dialogue about educational ends and means • variety of test formats can be used • testing can be incorporated into classroom instruction, maximizing student participation and motivation	• high opportunity cost to develop and validate test • faculty may not agree on test content • no point of comparison beyond institution • test security requires annual updating or large test item pool

- Standardized examinations may emphasize the lower-level objectives of Bloom's taxonomy (Chapter 6) rather than the current expanded definition of knowledge as the ability to apply and adapt concepts and principles.
- Testing with standardized instruments yields useful diagnostic information only if the test specifications correspond closely to program objectives, and if group subscores keyed to program objectives can be obtained.
- Results of a senior exit test cannot be used to benefit the students who take it, defeating a central purpose of assessment. Experience indicates (Jacobi, Astin, and Ayala, 1987; Johnson, 1993) that many students simply decline to participate in the assessment, regardless of incentives offered.

This section briefly summarizes procedures for developing or selecting knowledge outcome measures and analyzes options for obtaining information on knowledge outcomes. It also suggests ways to improve the usefulness of regular course examinations for program-level assessment.

9.2.1 Procedures for Developing Knowledge Outcome Measures

Expanded knowledge outcomes, as well as professionally-relevant skills, can be assessed using traditional "paper-and-pencil" measures and "performance" assessments. This section briefly summarizes procedures for the more traditional and familiar measures, while Section 9.3 focuses on performance assessment with emphasis on measuring intellectual, communication, and interpersonal skills.

The selection or development of knowledge outcome measures begins with a set of *objectives and performance criteria* as described in Chapter 7. The objectives should address the full range of *uses* of knowledge desired by the faculty, consistent with the expanded definition of knowledge needed in the new professional environment.

Using objectives and performance criteria greatly simplifies the task of designing measures. For knowledge outcomes, objectives will be translated into "objective" or "forced-choice" test items and "open-ended" or "free-response" items (for details of item construction and test design, see McBeath, 1992). While in principle objective tests can measure high-level cognitive outcomes, in practice it may be difficult to construct good forced-choice items to test these outcomes (Banta and Schneider, 1988). Fortunately, as noted earlier, some measures already used by faculty in their courses may be adaptable for purposes of program-level assessment. Sample materials for the full spectrum of knowledge and skill objectives can be found in curriculum resources such as the BYU report (1992) and USC's *Year 2000 Curriculum Project* (Diamond and Pincus 1994; Pincus, 1993), as well as in periodicals such as the *Journal of Accounting Education* and *Issues in Accounting Education*. Section 9.2.2 describes and evaluates various measurement options for knowledge outcomes.

When open-ended items are used, student responses should be rated on *performance criteria* developed by the faculty for the targeted objective(s). The development of performance criteria is described in Section 9.3. Faculty who use performance ratings should participate in rater training (also described in Section 9.3), whether they are applying the criteria for a course- or program-level evaluation.

Field testing or pilot testing is useful to prevent problems of unclear or inappropriate items or excessive test length. The instrument can be tested on a small group of students who have previously completed the relevant coursework and who would therefore not be part of the assessment sample. The validation sample should be similar to the group for which the measure is designed. No instrument should be used for the first time in a large-scale, high-stakes assessment.

Analyzing *reliability and validity* helps to interpret results of the pilot test and to determine whether the findings can be safely used to make generalizations about students' strengths, weaknesses, and overall performance on the objectives measured.

Modifications of the instrument will be suggested by analysis of pilot test results, reliability/validity data, discussion of results by the faculty, and review of students' feedback about the measure (obtained through discussion with students or using a brief questionnaire).

9.2.2 Options for Measuring Knowledge Outcomes

Options for measuring knowledge range from familiar course-embedded measures to formal achievement examinations and self-report data. By using a cluster of measures, faculty can balance the advantages and disadvantages of a single measure to obtain an overall portrait of students' strengths and weaknesses.

- *Course examinations and project grades* provide useful data to the extent these measures address targeted program objectives and produce subscores related to those objectives. This requirement can be met by compiling results for all students on each objective to create a profile of students' accomplishments.

  The value of examination scores for assessing aggregate performance of students increases when a common examination or item pool is used by all who teach the course, and when the test is demonstrated to be acceptably reliable and valid.

- *Course grades:* Grades in individual courses have limited usefulness as outcome measures because the basis for grading is not usually standardized. Grades include elements besides performance on knowledge tests, ranging from attendance and class participation to scores on group projects. Course grades can be made more informative as measures of learning outcomes by ensuring that they are based solely or primarily on students' performance relative to a specified subset of program objectives.

- *Grade-point averages (GPA):* Overall GPA is considered a moderately useful outcome measure by accounting program administrators (Chamberlain and others, 1991) and is widely used by employers of accounting graduates as well, as the following comment suggests:

Despite all the drawbacks of individual course grades, overall GPA does relate to job performance (and probably graduate school performance). It is a multi-year, multi-method, multi-rater measure and when used across institutions in the range we hire from, it works (Jean Wyer, personal communication, March 1994)

Although GPA "works" as a guide for employers, it is not useful as a diagnostic indicator for individual students nor does it provide useful information about program quality. GPA *is* a useful predictor for employers because of a partial overlap between the knowledge and skills assessed by some faculty and those needed for successful employment. GPA may also be a proxy indicator of non-academic skills that are needed for professional practice, for example, aggressiveness, the ability to navigate bureaucracies, and ability to organize one's time effectively (Peter Ewell, personal communication, March, 1994). The predictive validity of the GPA can be expected to be even greater when it reflects systematic assessment of students' performance on knowledge, skills, and values identified as central to professional success.

- *Achievement examinations* are designed to provide a cumulative assessment of knowledge retained by students. A risk is that the instrument may over-emphasize lower-level cognitive objectives for the sake of administrative convenience. As noted earlier, if the examination is given at the end of the senior year, the results are of little value to the students who take it. An achievement test designed to be administered late in the junior year can provide diagnostic information for both the program and students, again using the strategy of building the test around program objectives and providing subscores for each objective.

When using a standardized exam, test specifications should be examined closely to determine the degree of overlap with program objectives. Existing tests include:

CPA Exam: Although pass rates on the CPA exam are frequently used as an indicator of program quality, it is a licensure exam for public accounting, not a test of general achievement in accounting education. It is time-consuming and expensive, and because it is not required in order for graduates to practice accounting, self-selection bias precludes making judgments of program quality based on results. Moreover, it cannot be taken until students have graduated, nor does it provide subscores, so it cannot be used to provide timely diagnosis of students' strengths and weaknesses or to identify areas in the curriculum that may need attention (Herring and Izard, 1992). Thus, like GPA, the results may be useful for employers but have minimal value for program improvement.

Achievement Test for Accounting Graduates (ATAG): This examination (formerly the AICPA Level II Achievement Test) yields subscores in five areas (auditing, financial, cost and managerial, accounting information systems, and taxation) that correspond to basic divisions in the accounting curriculum at most institutions (Herring and Izard, 1992). However, Ingram and Petersen (1987) found that AICPA exam scores did not improve the predictive ability of regression models based on ACT scores and grades in lower-division accounting courses.

Other standardized exams: Other available instruments include the ACT Proficiency Examination Program in Accounting, designed for awarding credit by examination. The exam tests accounting proficiency at three levels, using objective and essay tests. ETS offers a course equivalency examination on Principles of Financial Accounting, designed for nontraditional students (Smith, Draper, and Bradley, 1994).

For more general assessment of business knowledge, the AACSB offers the Core Curriculum Assessment Program (CCAP). The CCAP is a data base which includes questions on accounting as well as other areas in the business curriculum. Schools may purchase the database on diskette and use it to design customized examinations. (Baker and other, 1993).

Instructor ratings: Checklists or narratives can be used to obtain judgments of students' knowledge and skills or of their performance in specific areas. While such judgments are subject to a number of sources of error (for example, "halo effects"), they offer a convenient way to obtain an estimate of students' strengths and weaknesses with respect to a particular category of outcomes.

Ratings are more reliable when they are based on specific performances such as oral or written examinations, presentations, projects, and simulations, and when the instructor or other rater has been trained to use agreed-upon performance criteria, as discussed in Section 9.3.

Student self-reports: Self-reports can provide a convenient profile of students' self-assessed strengths and weaknesses of both knowledge and skills. They can be used to gauge learning from specific instructional methods and materials (such as the multimedia resource, *Dermaceutics Inc.:* Risk Assessment and Planning; see example, Appendix 1). They can also be used to assess broad curricular outcomes. For example, several schools have devised questionnaires which ask seniors and alumni to judge their current level of knowledge and skill, based on AECC, FSA, or departmental objectives. Appendix 2 presents an example of a student self-report form from Arizona State University.

Advantages and Limitations: Self- and instructor-ratings have two important advantages: they can be obtained quickly and inexpensively, and they can be used to assess all major categories of learning outcomes: knowledge, skills, and values and attitudes.

Self-ratings are moderately correlated with other measures such as standardized examination scores but are not sufficiently valid to be used without other corroborating measures (Ewell, 1993). The problem is illustrated in an assessment of the *Dermaceutics* package mentioned above. Students in an experimental group studied audit concepts using the *Dermaceutics* package, while students in the control group participated in case discussions of extra problems and questions from the text. Experimental and control students did not differ significantly on *self-reported* understanding of the concepts. However, the actual *performance* of students in the experimental group was superior to that of the control group on multiple-choice and essay questions included on a mid-term examination (Mohrweis, 1993).

Because their validity is limited, self-report data should not be used to make placement or proficiency decisions, or other formal judgments about individual students. They are probably most useful for identifying potential problem areas. Checklists and other self-report measures may also facilitate students' discussions with their advisors about ways to improve their performance.

9.2.3 Improving the Quality of Knowledge Measures

Knowledge outcome measures can often be improved by following a few simple guidelines. Here are nine; others can be found in resources such as McBeath (1990), Erwin (1991), Ball State (n.d.) and references cited therein.

1. Prepare a test map indicating the objectives to be addressed and the weight given to each. Use to determine the number of items for each objective and points assigned to each.

2. Include the full range of knowledge outcomes in test specifications.
3. When using standardized tests, identify areas of overlap with program objectives as well as gaps in test coverage; compensate for the gaps and avoid drawing conclusions based on results for topics covered on the test but not included in the curriculum.
4. Observe basic rules for test item writing (for example, avoid double negatives, "all" or "none of the above," item stems that are too short or too vague).
5. Run a test analysis program to uncover weak items on objective tests.
6. Use strategies to minimize error when scoring essay tests, for example:
    *   Develop a scoring key; see, for example, Scofield and Combes (1993), reproduced in Appendix 3.
    *   Rate all responses to a single item in one pass, then shuffle the papers and rate all responses to the second item, and so on (to reduce contamination of scores and effects of order of presentation).
    *   Rate essays "blind," that is, ask students to put their names on the back of the paper or use a code.
7. Ask a colleague to review a draft of the test; see if your answers agree, and check for confusing wording.
8. Pilot test the instrument on a small sample of students; modify if necessary.
9. Use multiple measures to obtain a comprehensive picture of students' understanding of accounting concepts and principles and their use.

9.3 Measuring Skill Outcomes

Measuring complex skills such as problem solving, critical thinking, ethical reasoning, communication, and teamwork involves observing and making judgments about students' performance or the products of their efforts.

Performance measures are procedures and instruments that facilitate judgments made by qualified observers. These measures may be familiar to faculty who assign integrative projects such as written case studies, team projects, and oral presentations. For program-level assessment, performance measures can vary from impressionistic ratings of everyday behavior to formal assessments by trained raters reviewing students' written work or observing their performance in complex situations, such as a simulated client presentation or audit team planning meeting. Judgments can be made by faculty, graduate assistants, practicing professionals, and in some cases by students' peers.

Just as knowledge outcomes can be assessed using course-embedded measures, so too can data on students' intellectual, interpersonal, and communication skills be obtained by selectively compiling and anonymously *cross-grading* samples of work completed (and separately graded) as part of the normal instructional routine. Current practice favors course-embedded measures over logistically challenging alternatives external to normal coursework. Course-embedded measures are part of a trend toward integrating assessment with instruction to enhance its value to students and the ecological validity of measures used (Ewell, 1991b).

This section describes methods for obtaining performance measures and for increasing the validity and reliability of judgments of skill. Examples illustrate assessment of intellectual, interpersonal, and communication skills, and skills of learning to learn.

9.3.1 Procedures for Developing Performance Measures

The procedure for obtaining measures of performance is a slight variation of the procedure for measurement of knowledge outcomes outlined in Section 9.1.2:

- Review objectives and performance criteria and refine if necessary
- Develop scoring guide or rating scales for judging the product or performance, based on the performance criteria
- Define measurement situation for the target objective (presentation, simulation, project report, etc.)
- Observe performance or obtain product from students
- Rate or describe the performance or product using rating scale or scoring guide
- Compile results for review
- Recalibrate rating scale and/or revise measurement situation as needed

This section focuses on the use of performance criteria to develop rating scales or guidelines, selecting or defining measurement situations, and developing rater reliability.

9.3.1.1 Establishing Performance Criteria: For each major skill objective, criteria to judge the quality of performance must be identified, as described in Chapter 7. The criteria should be behaviorally explicit. For example, the ability to withstand and resolve conflict is an important objective recommended by the AECC under the category of interpersonal skills; it is also an important element of leadership. Performance criteria based on an established model of negotiation might specify that in a conflict situation the student:

- Identifies the source of the conflict
- Identifies principles to guide conflict resolution
- Maintains a focus on interests, not positions
- Actively explores the interests of all parties involved
- Acknowledges but does not react to emotions
- Actively explores options
- Seeks criteria of fairness for resolution (Fisher, Ury, and Patton, 1991)

Once identified, performance criteria such as these can be translated into guidelines or rating scales for measurement purposes as described below.

In addition to facilitating measurement, performance criteria serve a useful instructional purpose. When presented to students, they put forth a recognizable ideal toward which students can strive, and which can be discussed in concrete ways by students as they complete assigned projects and by faculty and students in teaching and advising situations. To reap these advantages, performance criteria should be made known to students early in the instructional process.

9.3.1.2 Defining the Measurement Strategy: The measurement strategy defines how evidence of students' achievement will be obtained. Sources of evidence for measurement of complex skills are of three general types:

- Judgments of a specific performance or product
- Judgments of ability
- Proxy indicators

Judgments of performance or product: As noted above, performance measures rely on observation or review of specific performances or products of student efforts such as oral presentations or examinations, written problems or case studies, performance in a team situation, or a portfolio of completed work from one or more courses. These performances must be judged by faculty or other qualified observers. Their judgments are usually expressed as ratings on performance criteria, or described in narrative evaluations.

Judgments of ability: Judgments of ability are based on observations of performance over time, for example, in a supervised internship or teamwork situation. Like judgments of specific performances or products, they may be expressed as ratings on performance criteria or as narrative evaluations. Requests for ability judgments can be incorporated into questionnaires administered to students, faculty, alumni, employers, or others who have opportunities to observe students' performance on the targeted objective(s) over time.

Proxy indicators provide indirect evidence that the targeted skill has been developed. For example, grades in a communication course could be used as an indicator of general communication skills. As emphasized in Section 9.2, the validity of grades as proxy indicators is greatest when the course is designed to teach specific objectives identified by the accounting faculty.

The measurement strategy consists of a *prompt* to initiate student performance, the performance situation or product to be evaluated, and the *instrument* used to codify reviewers' judgments. Instruments include the scoring guide or "rubric," rating scale, or guidelines for narrative descriptions of the product.

To illustrate, the prompt for a performance judgment might be a videotaped factory tour and client interview; the performance situation might be a discussion among students, acting as auditors reviewing the tour and interviewing clients to develop an audit plan (Mohrweis, 1993). Depending on the objective for which the assessment is intended, measurement could involve the use of ratings of individual students' effectiveness in the discussion (interpersonal and communication skills), ratings of the decisions reached by the group (decision-making), and/or scores on subsequent performance when asked to apply audit concepts (higher-level knowledge outcome). Alternatively, the prompt might be a complex accounting problem, the product to be judged being the students' analysis and solution proposals, rated using a scoring guide that emphasizes higher-level knowledge outcomes and problem-solving skills.

The concept of "authentic assessment" suggests that insofar as possible, measurement situations should reflect actual conditions of practice. The use of prompts such as complex cases and videotaped prompts depicting real-world situations lend authenticity to the assessment situation. Authenticity is enhanced when a real or hypothetical *purpose, audience* or client, and *context* are specified.

Examples of objectives, performance criteria, and measurement strategies for each of the major categories of skill categories identified in the AECC *Objectives* are given in Tables 9.2 through 9.8.

9.3.1.3 Developing Measurement Instruments: Judgments of performances or products can be expressed as numerical ratings or as narrative evaluations. As already noted, the performance criteria provide the foundation for developing an instrument such as a scoring guide or rating scale.

A scoring rubric can be designed to facilitate *holistic* or *analytical* judgments:

Holistic ratings are summary judgments of the product, performance, or ability viewed as a whole. Grades given to student projects exemplify holistic ratings: They summarize in a single letter or number, the degree to which each student's performance responds to the performance criteria. For example, a rating of "6" on a 6-point scale would mean that the students' work exemplified competence on virtually all of the criteria, while a rating of 2 would mean that very few of the criteria were met. Appendix 4 presents a six-point holistic scale to assess critical thinking skills (Facione and others, forthcoming).

Holistic ratings provide a *general* sense of how students are doing, but their diagnostic utility is limited since they do not allow faculty to compile a profile of students' strengths and weaknesses.

Analytical ratings are judgments based on each of the performance criteria taken in turn. They reflect *specific* characteristics of the desired product, performance, or ability. Separate ratings of the accuracy, organization, and supporting evidence in a case analysis illustrate the use of analytical ratings.

Analytical ratings are diagnostically useful because they enable faculty to identify patterns in students' performance as a group. For example, faculty review of a sample of case analyses performed by juniors might reveal that in general, students in the junior class receive higher subscores on accuracy of information than on the use of supporting evidence. Such results suggest relatively specific direction for follow-up assessment and curriculum development. The faculty may choose to review writing requirements, syllabi, assignments, and grading criteria to identify changes that could, for example, improve students' ability to use facts as evidence.

Occasionally, narrative descriptions of students' performance are preferable, for example, when preparing a dossier on which recommendations to employers or graduate programs will be based, or when the instrument is intended to foster students' self-assessment, as illustrated in Appendix 5. Narrative reports can also supplement numerical ratings.

Criteria identified for performance assessment should be made public and used throughout the curriculum to guide and reinforce students' efforts to develop targeted skills.

9.3.1.4 Qualifications of Raters: Whether made holistically or analytically, judgments of products, performances, and ability should be made by raters who are qualified based on their training, expertise, and opportunities for observation. Raters need not be "experts" in the domain of measurement; for example, it is *not* the case that only English teachers can judge the quality of students' writing. Raters, however expert, should participate in training to improve reliability of their judgments and agreement among judges (Section 9.3.1.5).

Although raters need not be "experts," colleagues with appropriate expertise (both academic and professional) are invaluable in developing effective measurement tasks based on performance criteria. Materials developed in consultation with these resource people can then be used by raters trained to apply the criteria, whether faculty, peers, graduate students, or practicing professionals. Training students to rate their own and each other's performance helps them develop self-assessment skills. Students' ratings will usually supplement rather than replace judgments of more experienced observers.

9.3.1.5 Improving Reliability of Qualitative Judgments: Measurement strategies used to assess complex skills generally rely on qualitative judgments of performance translated into numerical ratings or narrative descriptions, rather than quantitative measures such as frequency counts. The subjectivity inherent in qualitative judgments is often seen as a limitation of performance-based measures. However, use of a consensus-based training procedure reduces the subjectivity and increases the reliability of qualitative judgments. In this procedure, referred to here as rater training or "calibration" (of the rating instrument), individuals responsible for making judgments work together to develop consistency in judgment, that is, to improve *interrater reliability*.

Interrater reliability is a measure of the degree to which two independent raters agree on their judgments of performance on a defined task. Interrater reliability is expressed either as a correlation between two ratings or as the percent of cases on which raters' judgments fall within a specified range of agreement (for example, 70%-80% of judgments are within 1 point of each other on a 6-point scale). To develop interrater reliability, two or more raters will:

- Translate performance criteria into a rating scale, adapting the criteria as necessary to fit the specific performance or product to be rated
- Independently rate or describe samples of students' work drawn from the *same* pool of papers or performances that will be used for the final assessment
- Compare the ratings of all raters; discuss discrepancies until consensus is achieved
- Score a new sample; continue until the agreement criterion (for example, 75% of judgments by 2 independent raters are within one point of each other) is reached

Frequently, discussion of discrepancies between raters leads to clarification of the performance criteria or students' interpretation of the task. In this case it is advisable to revise the rating scale to more closely reflect the task.

When the agreement criterion is reached, raters score the remaining students' work independently. Often two raters score each sample; large discrepancies may be resolved by a third rater. Once reliability is firmly established, double ratings are generally not necessary, although periodic checks are advised when large numbers of the student sample must be rated (White, 1985). After scoring is completed, raters should debrief using questions such as the following:

- What strengths and weaknesses did students exhibit that were not reflected in the scoring rubric?
- Were there any patterns, for example in students' approach to the task, their understanding of the content, or their value orientations, that might have implications for the curriculum or instruction?
- Did you notice anything else that the scoring guide did not allow you to record? (adapted from Ewell, 1994, p. 43.)

Discussion of raters' observations is an important element in the ongoing review and revision of curriculum and instruction as well as the refinement of assessment materials. "Such discussions may in fact prove more important for encouraging improvement within a faculty team than the scores eventually assigned" (Ewell, 1994, p. 44).

Benefits: Rater training can be used to improve consistency of judgments about individual samples or portfolios of students' work, videotaped presentations, or other performance data. The procedure can also be incorporated into instruction to encourage students to develop self-assessment skills and the ability to make sound judgments about the performance of others (See Loacker and others, 1984, for examples). Application to assessment of writing portfolios is described in Belanoff and Elbow (1986).

Because cross-grading of students' work is time-consuming, it may be tempting to recruit independent judges, especially when the focus is on written or oral communication skills which faculty may not feel they are trained to judge. This tactic has the advantage of minimizing faculty time on assessment, but correspondingly limits faculty opportunities to develop a good diagnostic understanding of students' strengths and weaknesses as a basis for identifying instructional needs. Faculty involvement in developing and applying criteria also helps to clarify departmental standards, with likely benefits for departmental consistency in evaluating qualitative data such as papers, cases, and essay exams, all of which are likely to be more commonplace in accounting programs in the future.

At least in the formative stages of the assessment program, then, key faculty should participate in rating sessions so that the department can benefit from their systematic review of students' work.

9.3.2 Measuring Skills in the Accounting Curriculum

The strategies outlined above can be adapted to measure intellectual, communication, interpersonal, and learning-to-learn objectives of the accounting curriculum. Specific examples in each of these categories are provided below.

9.3.2.1 Intellectual Skills: Critical Thinking: Critical thinking may be defined as the open-minded investigation and analysis of a complex issue from a variety of perspectives, resulting in a well-supported position on the issue (Kurfiss, 1988). AECC *Objectives* related to critical thinking include inductive and deductive reasoning, critical analysis, and the "ability to present, discuss, and defend views effectively..." (p. 7).

Critical thinking is often measured using skills tests that focus on inductive and deductive reasoning, for example, the Watson Glaser Critical Thinking Appraisal, the Cornell Critical Thinking Test (Form Y, for college students), and the California Test of Critical Thinking Skills (CCTST, Facione, 1990a). These tests evaluate students' ability to use correct logical thinking and to avoid fallacies in reasoning about text passages, using a multiple-choice response format. Critical thinking tests tend to be correlated with measures of reading ability and both verbal and quantitative college entrance tests (MacMillan,1987; MacMillian & McPeck,1981; Facione, 1990b). Measures that rely on students' responses to open-ended prompts include the Ennis-Weir Critical Thinking Essay Test and subscales of the ACT-COMP instrument.

In practice, the skills of logical reasoning are necessary but not sufficient for critical thinking, largely because solving real-world problems depends on discipline-specific and even task-specific knowledge (Glaser, 1984). For example, a student's ability to argue the merits of a particular accounting method depends on knowledge of the options and how each is used (discipline-specific knowledge) and knowledge of the client's situation (task-specific knowledge), as well as the ability to relate general principles to the specific situation (deductive reasoning).

Skills of learning to learn (identified by Frances and others for the AECC, forthcoming) enable students to apply their knowledge to critical thinking tasks. Students must *question* the assumptions of all parties involved and the quality of the evidence for each position; they must *organize* relevant information to extract essential ideas; they must *connect* their knowledge to the concerns of various stakeholders in the controversy. They may also have to *adapt* their knowledge to generate novel alternatives. Lastly, to continue to develop their critical thinking skills, students must *reflect* on what they have learned from their investigations and from discussion of the issue with others who may not share their views. Assessment of learning-to-learn skills is discussed in section 9.4.2.

Assessment of critical thinking, then, should reflect its multifaceted character and dependence on adept use of professional knowledge. Case studies, simulations, and other performance assessments provide opportunities for students to demonstrate critical thinking skills in the accounting context.

Table 9.2 and Appendix 4 suggest criteria for evaluating students' performance on critical thinking tasks.

9.3.2.2 Intellectual Skills: Problem-Solving: Problem-solving involves the analysis of a situation in which a discrepancy exists between a current and desired state, development of alternative solutions, and formulation of an appropriate plan of action (Anderson, 1985).

The AECC *Objectives* include the "ability to identify and solve unstructured problems in unfamiliar settings and to apply problem-solving skills in a consultative process" (p. 7) among the essential outcomes of accounting education. Unstructured problems are those which require a search for information and generation of alternatives (Bonner and Walker, 1994). Like critical thinking, the solution of unstructured problems requires a blend of general problem-solving ability, knowledge, and learning-to-learn skills.

Problem-solving and critical thinking are closely related cognitive processes. Both involve analytical reasoning, induction, deduction, a search for evidence, and synthesis of ideas into a complex whole. Both require professionally-relevant knowledge and application of learning-to-learn skills. They differ primarily in their focus:

- Critical thinking is use of cognitive processes to develop and support a point of view on an issue
- Problem-solving is use of cognitive processes to analyze and resolve a troublesome situation (Kurfiss, 1988)

For example, critical thinking is involved when students are asked to identify the issues associated with a substantial cost over-run on a contract for new, technologically sophisticated equipment, and to analyze those issues. Complex problem-solving is involved when the students are asked to propose a solution. Critical thinking is involved when students are asked to interpret financial information for an institution that has made some fraudulent transactions and is now on the verge of bankruptcy; complex problem-solving is emphasized when students must develop options and recommend a course of action to restructure the company, including raising new capital.

Problem-Solving in Accounting: The AICPA practice analysis described in Chapter 6 delineates tasks and activities related to accounting and auditing and to taxation compliance, consultation, and representation. The AICPA's outline of procedures may be viewed as a guide for approaching the general problem of assessing and completing an engagement. The tasks in accounting and auditing are presented in Figure 6.1 (Chapter 6).

Accounting graduates must be prepared to respond effectively to unusual circumstances and problems that may arise in each phase of an engagement. Performance criteria for problem-solving, presented below, suggest a model for the teaching and assessment of problem-solving skills in accounting.

Performance Criteria for Problem-Solving Skills: Problem-solving ability may be judged according to performance criteria such as the following:

- Identifying and diagnosing the problem (clarifying the circumstances that make the situation a problem for the client; identifying constraints; determining client's goals; identifying and ranking possible courses of action; recognizing the limits of what is known and costs of obtaining additional information; and establishing the optimal timetable for resolution of the problem)
- Generating alternative solutions and strategies (identifying possible solutions to the problem; clarifying possible means to achieve each of the potential solutions; and determining limitations on each potential solution)
- Developing a plan of action (identifying the full spectrum of possible plans of action; evaluating the relative merits of each possible plan; and tentatively settling on a plan)
- Implementing the plan (determining who should implement the plan, establishing the optimal timetable for completion, and monitoring and revising the plan)
- Keeping the planning process open to new information and ideas (quoted with modifications from MacCrate, 1992, pp. 129-135)

In addition to the processes indicated above, problem-solving and critical thinking in accounting often involve identification of ethical issues. Although ethical reasoning skills are discussed separately below, they can often be assessed in conjunction with both problem-solving and critical thinking tasks.

Sample performance criteria and indicators for measuring problem-solving abilities in the accounting context are provided in Table 9.3.

9.3.2.3 Intellectual Skills: Ethical Reasoning: The AECC *Objectives* includes among the important intellectual skills the ability to identify ethical issues and make well-founded ethical judgements and decisions in the context of accounting practice. Professional accountants - both public and corporate - routinely face ethical dilemmas (Finn and others, 1988). Ethical issues faced by accountants range from fulfilling a broad responsibility to society to the detection of fraud, and from forming an opinion on financial presentations to reporting illegal acts. Incorporating ethical issues into the curriculum, and assessing students' ability to identify ethical dilemmas/questions and to apply a value-based reasoning system, communicates that the faculty places a high priority on professional ethics.

Performance Criteria: Performance criteria for ethical reasoning include the ability to analyze the role of the professional accountant in ethically challenging situations, to articulate ethical dilemmas implicit within a case or real-world problem, to identify the stakeholders in the situation, and to apply a specific ethical framework (such as utilitarianism, rights, justice or virtue ethics) to analysis of the problem and development of solution proposals (Velasquez, 1992).

Measurement options: Ethical reasoning skills can be assessed using students' written or oral case presentations or observation of simulations that involve ethical issues. Ratings can be made by faculty, peers, and/or professional accountants. Cases can include dilemmas that are relatively straightforward (such as fraud) or more subtle (such as a request by a client to choose accounting methods to minimize taxes or influence stock prices).

Another option for measuring ethical reasoning is a research instrument called the Defining Issues Test (DIT). This instrument identifies the considerations people use to make judgments when confronted with moral dilemmas (Rest, 1990). For example, some individuals base their judgments on fear of punishment, others on the desire to conform to social norms, still others on the wish to obey the letter of the law, and others on the basis of "universal" ethical principles such as honesty. According to the underlying theory (Kohlberg, 1976), each of these considerations is associated with a different "stage" of moral reasoning, with universal ethical principles presumed to represent the highest stage. The DIT, or an adaptation of it to an accounting context, could be used to determine the issues students use to reason about ethical dilemmas. Because the DIT asks students to rank-order ethical criteria, it may also be used to measure professional attitudes and values (Section 9.4).

The DIT has been used to compare accounting majors to students in other majors (Jeffrey, 1993; St. Pierre, Nelson, and Gabbin, 1990), in experimental studies of ethics interventions in accounting (Ponemon, 1993) and in business programs generally (Conry and Nelson, 1989). A related approach using simplified criteria and focused on the professional accounting environment is presented in Hiltebeitel and Jones (1991).

Sample performance criteria, indicators and measurement options for ethical reasoning skills in an accounting context are provided in Table 9.4.

9.3.2.4 Interpersonal Skills: Interpersonal skills enable students and graduates to work effectively with others as clients, co-workers, or government officials; in day-to-day interactions, in teamwork situations, or in negotiations. Interpersonal skills include:

- Social skills (such as conveying warmth and working compatibly with others)
- Task-oriented skills (such as helping to achieve consensus)
- Linguistic skills (such as presenting ideas clearly)
- Analytical skills (such as the ability to analyze interpersonal dynamics and apply the analysis to facilitate constructive interaction) (adapted from Bayer, 1993, and BYU Core, Vol. II, 1992)

Interpersonal vs. Communication Skills: Although interpersonal skills overlap in important ways with communication skills, communication skills are most often assessed in formal situations in which the individual or group presents a product (such as a presentation, written examination or paper). In contrast, interpersonal skills are those called into play while *creating* the product or working with others to achieve a goal.

Value of Teaching and Assessing Interpersonal Skills: Interpersonal skills are frequently cited as important for accounting graduates' chances of professional success, offering a compelling reason to include these skills in the program's goals and the assessment portfolio. However, teaching and assessing interpersonal skills requires a greater departure from customary practice in accounting education than the teaching and assessment of intellectual and communication skills. Faculty in the accounting program may feel that they do not have the expertise to teach such skills, so that assessing them in the accounting context is not appropriate.

Nonetheless, incorporating interpersonal skills into the curriculum and its assessment adds an important dimension of quality to the program. Emphasis on this aspect of students' development invites use of active learning and authentic assessment strategies in which students try out professional roles and learn to take the perspectives of future co-workers, managers, clients, IRS agents and the like. Formulating explicit criteria for assessment of interpersonal skills will increase faculty awareness of opportunities to reinforce these skills, while offering benchmarks to students for self-assessment and self-improvement.

Performance Criteria for Interpersonal Skills: Performance criteria for assessing teamwork, one form of interpersonal skills, should reflect behaviors that facilitate effective functioning of the group. Examples from the BYU Core (Vol. II, 1992) include:

- Exhibits a positive disposition to the task at hand
- Comes to group sessions prepared
- Completes assigned tasks on a timely basis

Additional criteria to consider include:

- Contributes actively and appropriately
- Facilitates contributions of others
- Helps to achieve group goals while maintaining positive relationships
- Accurately assesses group process and provides behavioral feedback in a form acceptable to the group

The functioning of the group as a unit can also be assessed, either by student participants, peer observers, or faculty, for example in a post-task debriefing session or using a brief rating scale. For example, members of an effective group can be expected to work together to:

- Establish manageable goals
- Clarify roles and expectations
- Establish ground rules
- Develop open communication
- Resolve conflict
- Develop consensus (Bayer, 1993)

Feedback on group functioning should be discussed by the group to foster both individual and team learning (Johnson, Johnson, and Smith, 1990). The *product* of the group's efforts can also be assessed using criteria appropriate to the task.

Measurement Strategies for Interpersonal Skills: Interpersonal skills (including teamwork) can be measured by:

- Instructor observation and rating of interpersonal interactions (live, videotaped)
- Peer ratings of individual contributions to group process
- Employer or internship supervisor ratings
- Instructor ratings of students' analysis of interpersonal and team situations (proxy measure)

Since observation and rating of students' behavior provide the most direct basis for judging interpersonal skills, peers are often in the best position to judge interpersonal skills.

Peers as raters: Peer ratings are both practical and appropriate in measuring interpersonal and team skills when coursework includes group projects, presentations, or problem-solving activities. Before using a rating scale, the instructor should conduct a practice session in which students use the scale to rate videotaped interactions and discuss their ratings (similar to a reliability training session). Although the discussion is focused on use of the rating scale, it also serves an instructional purpose by directing students' attention to effective and ineffective interpersonal and team behavior.

Effective use of peer ratings: Using peer ratings may create anxiety about evaluation. Students are often reluctant to evaluate their peers, so the instructor should clarify the rationale and explain how the information will be used. The instructor can also remind students that professionals are often called upon to evaluate co-workers. Peer ratings should be treated by the instructor as advisory, that is, to supplement the instructor's own judgments and to aid in diagnosing strengths and weaknesses in students' interpersonal abilities.

Appendix 6 illustrates a peer rating form that combines ratings of group skills, leadership, and conflict resolution (BYU Core, Vol. II, 1992).

- *Faculty as raters:* Although faculty may be reluctant to judge students' interpersonal skills, use of rating criteria can simplify the task. In large classes, it is difficult for faculty to acquaint themselves with interpersonal skills of individual students. Videotapes of students working in groups can facilitate observation. Faculty can also observe students working in groups during class. However, unless the professor observes groups at work over a period of time, ratings will have little reliability or validity.
- *Analytical measures:* Faculty may elect to judge students' ability to analyze actual or hypothetical interpersonal situations as a proxy measure of interpersonal skills. Although the ability to analyze interpersonal transactions does not necessarily mean one can handle them in practice, focusing students' attention on interpersonal dynamics provides them with tools they can later use in actual practice situations.

Tables 9.5 and 9.6 suggest strategies and criteria for measuring teamwork and conflict resolution skills. Like other performance measures described in this document, the measures suggested here can be incorporated into classroom instruction to facilitate data collection.

9.3.2.5 Communication Skills: Communication skills are those abilities that enable individuals to convey information and ideas to others and to understand the information and ideas others present to them. Professional accountants must be able to discuss technical information with clients and co-workers as well as establish rapport with clients by carrying on informal conversation. Specific skills include the ability to (Greenberg and Smith, pp. 244-245):

- Ask appropriate questions to determine clients' needs and to obtain necessary information
- Answer clients' questions
- Write coherent memos and letters to the IRS, clients and co-workers

Oral and written communication skills learned in courses outside the accounting curriculum should be applied and reinforced in accounting courses to ensure transfer of those skills to professional situations.

When communication skills are evaluated as an integral part of assignments in accounting, the professional relevance of those skills is conveyed unequivocally to students. The message is amplified when attention given to these skills in individual courses is reinforced by program-level assessments such as reviews of portfolios of students' work.

Performance Criteria for Communication Skills: Performance criteria for communication skills depend on the particular aspect of communication to be emphasized. For example, listening skills, identified as important in the AECC statement of objectives, are frequently judged on the basis of the listener's ability to identify the main points in an oral communication and to judge the purpose or intent of the communication. Other criteria for "listening" include formulating questions to obtain additional needed information or the identification of underlying feelings without reacting emotionally oneself.

An important communication objective identified in the AECC *Objectives* is the "ability to present, discuss, and defend views effectively through formal and informal, written and spoken language" (p. 7). In this formulation, the medium of communication is secondary to the ability to present and support ideas (often categorized as the intellectual skill of critical thinking, discussed above). Performance criteria for this aspect of communication skill could require the student to:

- Clearly state a position on the topic
- Organize the presentation in terms of a few main points or themes
- Choose appropriate illustrations, examples, or evidence to support his or her position
- Use a level of detail appropriate to the audience's needs and interests (Loacker and others, 1984; Ewell, 1988)

When the focus is on oral communication of ideas, it may be important to emphasize the ability not only to defend ideas but to engage in effective dialogue with others. The following performance criteria have been suggested:

- Identifies the main points of oral statements by others
- Identifies points of agreement and disagreement in an oral exchange
- Modifies his or her own arguments in light of new information (Ewell, 1988)

Measurement Strategies for Communication Skills: Opportunities to observe and assess oral communication skills are numerous when the accounting program encourages active student involvement in learning. Formal class presentations, case discussions, role play situations, oral examinations, and conferences with the professor require students to communicate orally in an accounting context. Similarly, written case studies, memoranda, client letters, position papers, research papers, and group and individual projects serve as windows on written communication skills while enabling faculty to assess students' mastery of accounting concepts and their application. Oral presentations can be videotaped for later review and critique by the student and instructor, or for cross-rating by program faculty as part of a program-level assessment.

Accounting programs have incorporated assessment of written and oral communication skills in varying degrees. For example, at Brigham Young University, students write numerous papers, give presentations in a variety of settings, and take oral final examinations. A standardized rating sheet is used by faculty to assess both content (adapted to the specific presentation topic) and communication skills in formal written and oral presentations. BYU faculty assess listening skills using exercises that involve following verbal instructions, summarizing a videotaped presentation, and self-diagnosis (BYU, 1992, Vol. 2). Scofield (1994) lists characteristics of oral presentations (Appendix 7). These characteristics can readily be adapted for use as performance criteria and translated into a rating scale.

The use of standardized rating scales to assess communication (and other skills) throughout the curriculum serves two important functions. In addition to providing very specific and consistent feedback to students, rating scales allow the faculty periodically to aggregate results for each of the performance criteria to determine whether students show patterns of strengths and weaknesses and whether skills show improvement over time. Care should be taken to ensure that any widely-used rating scales adequately reflect the desired outcomes and performance criteria. Reliability of ratings should be checked periodically using procedures described in Section 9.3.

For particular assignments, an instructor can supplement departmental rating scales tailored to the assignment. This method allows the instructor to assess both communication skills and application of knowledge. For example, Scofield and Combes (1993) describe a writing assignment in which students must prepare two alternative balance sheets and write a memorandum to the CEO recommending one of the two formats. Goals of the assignment include:

- The student will use official pronouncements
- The student will recognize conflicts within current GAAP
- The student will place accounting in its business context
- The student must make an accounting decision (pp. 78-79)

Appendix 3, mentioned earlier, presents the assignment, criteria and checklist used to facilitate scoring of this assignment.

9.4 Measuring Professional Orientation: Values and Attitudes

Professional orientation refers to the values, attitudes, and behaviors that reflect an individual's identification with and respect for the accounting profession. Values are "the important and stable ideas, beliefs, and assumptions that affect our behaviors" (Fuhrmann and Grasha, p. 22). Criteria for determining an individual's value commitments include:

- Choosing the targeted value freely from among examined alternatives
- Affirming the value publicly
- Acting consistently and repeatedly in accordance with the value (adapted from Raths and others, 1966; Fuhrmann and Grasha, 1983)

Evidence of values and attitudes can be obtained by observing students' and graduates' voluntary behavior (choosing and acting) and by self-reports of preferences, agreement, and behavior (choosing, affirming, and acting). This discussion presents:

- A brief introduction to measurement of values and attitudes
- Suggestions for measurement of four aspects of professional orientation drawn from the AECC's *Objectives,* using the framework of choosing, affirming, and acting consistently

9.4.1 Measurement Strategies for Values and Attitudes

Many strategies for measuring values and attitudes are familiar to faculty. Examples include:

- Observer judgments of actions in simulations, internships, or other performance situations
- Content analysis of focus group discussions
- Participation rates in activities related to targeted values and attitudes
- Students' ratings of agreement with statements of values and attitude
- Students' self-reports of relevant behavior

As in measurement of knowledge and skills, the measurement of values and attitudes depends on a clear statement of objectives. Procedures for developing interrater reliability, described in Section 9.3, should be applied when using observer judgments, rating scales, and focus groups to assess professional attitudes and values. Participation rates can be obtained through various unobtrusive measurement strategies such as head-counts or sign-in logs at department-sponsored programs. Ratings of agreement with value statements require statements that are written to minimize the influence of social desirability. Students' self-reported behavior can provide relatively reliable data although validation of all such instruments is always advisable.

Pitfalls in Assessment of Values and Attitudes: In general, it is better to base judgments of values and attitudes on what people do rather than on what they say, since individuals can understand and affirm a value without acting upon it. Thus individuals may recognize an ethical situation, analyze the situation using valid ethical frameworks, and identify the morally correct response, yet lack the moral will to act on their analysis by refraining from unethical conduct (such as plagiarism or cheating) (Rest, 1986; Conry and Nelson, 1989). Similarly, students may describe themselves as open to diversity (affirming), yet fail to notice that they avoid working in group situations with peers from ethnic or racial groups other than their own (choosing, acting).

The challenge, then, in measuring values and attitudes is to *identify the kinds of behavior most likely to reflect the existence of the desired value or attitude.* Because it is not always possible to measure behavior, self-report instruments must frequently be used. When using self-report data, multiple measures can be used to strengthen conclusions. Validating self-report instruments using criterion measures also strengthens the basis for drawing conclusions based on their results.

9.4.2 Measuring Values and Attitudes in the Accounting Curriculum

In the *Objectives,* the AECC identifies three central outcomes related to professional orientation:

- Lifelong learning (p. 6)
- Professional integrity: ethics and judgment (pp. 2-3)
- Personal capacities and attitudes (p. 8)

The *Objectives* also suggests an underlying capacity that integrates knowledge, skills, and values:

- Learning to learn

This section suggests measurement strategies for each of these four outcome categories, using the framework of choosing, affirming, and acting consistently as it applies to accounting situations.

9.4.2.1 Lifelong Learning: As defined by the AECC, an attitude of lifelong learning is essential for learning to learn. This attitude, as described in the *Objectives,* has two major components:

- Valuing continual improvement of self and profession
- Welcoming, "even thriving on, uncertainty and unstructured situations" (p. 6)

Continual improvement of self and profession: Students who value continual self-improvement can be expected to *choose* activities that support personal and professional growth, to *publicly affirm* the importance of such activities and their intention to engage in them in the future, and to demonstrate a consistent pattern of *acting* on their intentions over an extended period of time. Phrased as a specific program objective, this value might be stated as follows:

The student actively seeks out and affirms the value of opportunities for continual learning, self-improvement, and improvement of the profession.

Indicators that students value continual improvement might include:

- Participation in faculty research or membership in student chapters of professional organizations (choosing, acting)
- Self-reported plans to remain professionally active after graduation (affirming)
- Agreement with statements in support of lifelong learning (affirming)

The Locus of Learning Motivation Scale, reproduced in Appendix 8, is a self-report measure of commitment to lifelong learning values (Nelson, 1992).

Table 9.7 illustrates a measurement plan for the goal of continual improvement of self and profession. Note that not all students are expected to participate in all activities, but that some participation by all (or some designated percentage of) students may be a realistic *program* goal.

Welcoming uncertainty and unstructured situations: Section 9.3 describes methods for measuring the *skills* required to make decisions in unstructured situations, for example, critical thinking, problem solving, and teamwork. The AECC *Objectives* emphasizes that students must also develop an *attitude* of accepting and thriving on the challenges of unstructured situations. A relevant objective would be:

The student actively seeks out and affirms the value of opportunities to solve unstructured problems and to work in unstructured situations.

Applying the criteria for assessment of values, the student who welcomes uncertainty and unstructured situations might be expected to:

- Demonstrate a preference for instructional methods that involve unstructured situations, for example, the case method, simulations, and collaborative learning

- Go beyond assignments to consider implications (choosing, affirming)
- Consistently seek out opportunities to work in complex, unstructured situations, for example, choose an internship in a start-up company (choosing, acting)

Available instruments: Several existing instruments assess attitudes and values relevant to students' receptiveness to uncertainty and unstructured situations.

Learning Styles: The preference for unstructured situations is related to several widely-used models of students' approach to learning. For example, the Myers-Briggs Type Indicator (MBTI) includes a scale, the Sensing/Intuiting dimension, that could be used to assess students' preference for structured or unstructured situations (choosing, affirming). Students who score high on the Sensing mode tend to prefer concrete detail and well-structured, practical learning involving the use of direct application of rules and procedures, while students who score high on the Intuitive mode are more likely to be comfortable with ambiguity, abstractions, hypothetical situations, and less-structured learning situations. Accounting majors generally prefer the Sensing mode (Geary and Rooney, 1993; see also Schroeder, 1993).

Intellectual development: The model of intellectual development developed by William Perry, Jr., characterizes students along dimensions of structure, uncertainty, and reliance on authority. An instrument with direct application to the classroom is the Educational Environment Preferences scale (LEP), which assesses students' preferences for structured or unstructured learning situations, based on Perry's model (Moore, 1987).

Dispositions toward Critical Thinking: The Critical Thinking Dispositions Inventory (CCTDI) assesses students' tendency to endorse values related to learning in unstructured situations, for example open-mindedness, inquisitiveness, systematic and analytical thinking, truth-seeking (attention to evidence), and the need to make judgments in the face of uncertainty (Facione, Sanchez, Facione, and Gainen, forthcoming).

9.4.2.2 Professional Integrity: A second key dimension of professional orientation is professional integrity. Central to professional integrity is the ethical dimension, which includes three characteristics identified by the AECC: understanding of the ethics of the profession, the ability to make value-based judgments, and a disposition "to address issues with...concern for the public interest" (*Objectives*, pp. 2-3).

Technical knowledge of the ethics of the profession can be assessed by examination, but professional integrity requires the disposition to *apply* ethical principles in specific, real-world situations. As noted in Section 9.4.3, ethical reasoning is often assessed using the Defining Issues Test (Rest, 1990); this instrument may also provide insight regarding the values chosen by students and graduates, since it requires them to rank-order values.

Cases and dilemmas that involve an ethical dimension offer opportunities to observe and judge students' commitment to the ethics of the profession. Students' responses can be rated for recognition of the ethical dimension of the case, appropriate application of ethical principles of the profession, and the value orientation reflected in their decisions.

A simplified rating scale is suggested by research on the impact of integrating ethics into the accounting curriculum (Hiltebeitel and Jones, 1991). In this research, students read brief dilemmas related to personal and professional issues arising in the workplace, then rank the importance of six criteria that could be used to resolve the dilemma. The criteria are:

a. My personal integrity
b. Keeping my job
c. The respect of my peers
d. Legal responsibility
e. Professional responsibility
f. Getting promoted

Options b, c, and f are considered to reflect lower-level moral stages than items a, d, and e (based on Kohlberg's theory of moral development; 1976). This method adapts the strategy on which the Defining Issues Test is based (discussed in Section 9.4) to the professional context with emphasis on accounting situations. Although these criteria are quite general, they were sufficient to discriminate between treatment and control groups in the experiment. The criteria can be modified or extended to include other aspects of professional ethics, for example concern for the public interest.

As noted earlier, however, such measures are at best proxies for actual behavior, and results may not be consistent with students' actions. An experiment in an auditing course demonstrates how this discrepancy can be used for both instruction and assessment. The researchers returned examinations with false grades, some 10 points over, some 10 points under, and some with no change. Nearly all students in the group which had points deducted reported an error, but no students in the other two groups reported errors. The researchers note that reporting the results of this experiment to the class increased motivation to discuss issues of integrity in auditing and management (Dirsmith and Ketz, 1987).

In addition to the ethical dimension of professional integrity, the *Objectives* suggest that graduates "should be prepared to address issues with integrity, objectivity and competence." As with other aspects of professional orientation, these attitudes can be assessed using ratings by peers and faculty, judgments of internship supervisors and employers, and in some cases, attitude scales.

Students' attitudes toward objectivity can be measured using the CCTDI (Truth-seeking and Open-mindedness Scales), mentioned above; this instrument also measures attitudes toward several important dimensions of professional competence, notably, analytical and systematic thinking and the willingness to suspend judgment (Maturity subscale) (Facione and others, forthcoming).

9.4.2.3 Personal Capacities and Attitudes: In addition to its special emphasis on lifelong learning, the AECC *Objectives* identifies the following important "personal capacities and attitudes":

• Creative thinking
• Integrity
• Energy
• Motivation
• Persistence
• Empathy
• Leadership
• Sensitivity to social responsibilities (pp. 6 and 8)

These capacities are difficult to judge, but can be inferred from the extent and quality of students' participation in the academic program and related educational experiences. Again, faculty, peer, and supervisor ratings can be compiled to obtain a profile of students and graduates on these dimensions. An example is the assessment of students' *sensitivity to social responsibility*. An objective based on this outcome might be stated as follows:

Students will exhibit social responsibility in professionally relevant contexts.

Performance criteria could include voluntary involvement in professionally-related community service activity, voluntary expression of socially responsible attitudes in class discussions, and inclusiveness and sensitivity in teamwork situations. Indicators such as self-reports and observational data can provide information relevant to this objective as to others.

Professional orientation should also include a positive attitude toward the accounting profession. A widely-used, validated measure of attitudes toward the profession is the Accounting Attitude Scale (AAS; Nelson, 1992; see Appendix 9). A variation of the AAS yielded substantial changes in agreement ratings on several items after a new curriculum was implemented at Arizona State University. For example, at the end of the first year of the new program, students showed higher levels of disagreement with the statement, "Accountants are number-crunchers" who "seldom work with people" (McKenzie, 1993). Attitude change of this nature may help to recruit a more diverse population of students to the profession, and may serve as an indicator of students' motivation to persist in the profession.

9.5 Learning to Learn: Integrating Knowledge, Skills, and Professional Orientation

In addition to knowledge and performance-oriented outcomes, the *Objectives* emphasize the need for accounting graduates to develop skills and attitudes that will provide a foundation for continued learning when they enter the professional arena. The authors of the *Objectives* refer to this important cluster of outcomes as "learning to learn," with the ultimate aim being the capacity for lifelong learning.

The model of learning to learn outlined in the *Objectives* has three components:

• Foundational understanding of content
• Inquiry-oriented learning processes and skills
• "An **attitude** of continual inquiry" and comfort with uncertainty

Foundational Understanding of Content: The authors of the *Objectives* recognize that developing the capacity for lifelong learning implies that students must learn program content (principles and concepts) in conjunction with "the ability to apply and adapt those concepts and principles in a variety of contexts and circumstances." The perspective of lifelong learning implies a broad definition of what is assessed, extending beyond traditional concepts of measuring memorized rules and regulations to include the full range of knowledge outcomes defined in Chapter 6.

Inquiry-oriented Learning Processes and Skills: The *Objectives* underscore "the process of inquiry in an unstructured environment" as a central part of learning to learn. Specific skills students must acquire include "the ability to identify problems and opportunities, search out the desired information, analyze and interpret the information, and reach a well reasoned conclusion." (p. 6) These skills are closely related to critical thinking and problem solving as defined in Section 9.3.2.

Attitude of Continual Inquiry: Learning to learn depends upon an attitude of willingness, even eagerness to learn; the *Objectives* emphasize an attitude of thriving on uncertainty, continual inquiry, and continual self-improvement. Assessment of these lifelong-learning values is described in the previous section.

Learning skills that underlie the capacities outlined here are embodied in the model of an "intentional learner," proposed by Francis, Mulder, and Stark in a monograph in preparation for the AECC. These researchers have isolated five key skills of learning to learn:

- Questioning
- Organizing
- Connecting
- Reflecting
- Adapting

The forthcoming monograph describes ways in which the curriculum can foster the development of these skills, but discusses assessment of these skills only briefly. Table 9.8 suggests performance criteria and measurement strategies relevant to each of the five learning-to-learn skills.

9.6 Conclusion: The Challenges of Measuring Learning Outcomes

Developing valid and reliable performance-based measures of learning outcomes is a challenging task, although one with many familiar elements for faculty who assign individual and team projects, cases, preparation and analysis of financial statements, and other multi-dimensional tasks as part of instruction. Refining measures currently in use, and developing shared criteria for judging students' work, are useful ways to establish a system of measurement for program-level assessment.

In addition to describing measures for expanded knowledge outcomes and performance measures, this chapter has suggested strategies for measuring "professional orientation," which includes values and attitudes as they relate to professional integrity and the motivation to pursue lifelong learning. Some may argue that attitudes and values can neither be taught nor assessed, and do not fall within the sphere of educational responsibility occupied by the accounting program. Nonetheless, any academic program does communicate values and attitudes, for example, through curricular emphasis, what the faculty evaluates and rewards, how students perceive that faculty allocate their time, and through the quality of day-to-day interactions among students, faculty, staff, employers, and the general public. Explicit attention to these dimensions in the assessment program reinforces their importance in the eyes of the faculty and conveys to students the expectations of both the academic and professional communities.

Consulting with experts on assessment of particular skills (e.g., writing, speaking, ethics and values) can be useful in the initial stages of developing or refining measurements, for example, to help faculty articulate performance criteria and identify cost-effective ways to obtain information of value to them. Equally important is involvement of practicing professionals. Finally, the greatest benefits of measurement are likely to come when faculty examine students' work collectively—not only from the familiar perspective of judging individual performance but also from the perspective of how well students, taken as a whole and in appropriate subgroups, meet faculty expectations and are prepared to meet the needs of a dynamically changing profession.

TABLE 9.1
SAMPLE GOALS, OBJECTIVES, AND POSSIBLE INDICATORS:
AN OVERVIEW

Goals[a]	Objectives[b] and Performance Criteria[c]	Sample Indicators[d]
Problem-solving ability	Graduating seniors will be able to identify and solve unstructured real-world problems to the satisfaction of faculty and corporate evaluators	Students' performance on written analyses of complex case studies
Communication skills	Graduating seniors will be able to present, discuss, and defend their views effectively through formal and informal, written and spoken language	Students' performance on a series of formal and informal, written and spoken presentations and discussions of their views on topics related to accounting
Manage challenging pressures	Graduating seniors will be able to select and assign priorities with restricted resources and organize work to meet tight deadlines	Students' performance on in-basket exercise Faculty ratings of students' organizational ability (e.g., timely completion of class projects and assignments)

[a]Goals: What general competencies will students acquire?
[b]Objectives: What action will students be able to perform as a result of instruction?
[c]Performance Criteria: What characteristics will define acceptable performance?
[d]Indicators/Evidence: How will an observer know students have achieved the objective? (Adapted from Ewell, 1988).

TABLE 9.2
MEASUREMENT OPTIONS FOR INTELLECTUAL SKILL:
CRITICAL THINKING

Objective: Students will demonstrate the ability to think critically and analytically about controversial subjects in the field of accounting.

Performance Criteria	Indicators/Evidence:
Student formulates the issue clearly and succinctly	Ratings (using criteria at left) of position papers, memoranda, oral presentations etc., compiled in a portfolio for review by faculty and/or practicing professionals
Student identifies alternative perspectives on the issue	
Student obtains and evaluates evidence in support of each perspective	Ratings by faculty of individual student's contributions to class discussions about controversial subjects in accounting
Student clearly articulates a position on the issue (orally or in writing)	Student self-assessments of strengths and weaknesses on criteria, obtained through questionnaires
Student uses evidence persuasively to support the position chosen	Employer ratings of graduate's skill in critical and analytical thinking
Student takes into account strengths of opposing positions	
Student uses correct logical reasoning throughout the presentation	

TABLE 9.3
MEASUREMENT PLAN FOR INTELLECTUAL SKILL
GOAL: PROBLEM-SOLVING

Objective: Students will be able to identify and solve unstructured real-world problems drawn from accounting practice.

Performance Criteria	Indicators/Evidence:
Student identifies central problem(s) in a complex situation drawn from accounting practice	Cross-grading of written case analyses using analytical rating scale based on performance criteria (listed at left)
Student recognizes multiple causal factors involved in a problem situation	Ratings of senior projects by faculty and/or practicing professionals
Student uses systems thinking to analyze the problem	Ratings of memos, technical reports, or other writing produced in simulated practice situation involving problem analysis and solution
Student correctly uses accounting principles to address the problem	
Student generates plausible alternative solutions to address the problem	Employer ratings of intern's or graduate's problem-solving ability
Student offers persuasive reasons and evidence in support of solution proposal	Observer ratings of student engaged in group problem-solving exercise
Student adapts solutions to unexpected new information	

TABLE 9.4

MEASUREMENT PLAN FOR ETHICAL REASONING

Objective (AECC): Students will be able to identify ethical issues and apply a value-based reasoning system to ethical questions.

Performance Criteria	Indicators/Evidence:
Student articulates ethical dilemmas of practice in an ill-defined accounting situation	Faculty ratings (using criteria at left) of written or oral responses to videotaped or written case presentations
Student identifies key stakeholders in the situation and their responsibility to the public	Ratings of student's ethical awareness, analysis, and decision-making in live or videotaped simulations
Student applies more value-based frameworks to analyze the situation	Global ratings of student's responses in class discussions of ethical issues
Student offers a fair, equitable, and responsible solution proposal	Employer ratings of graduate's skill in addressing ethical issues
Student effectively supports the proposed decision or course of action using ethical grounds	

TABLE 9.5

MEASUREMENT PLAN FOR INTERPERSONAL SKILLS

Objective: Students will be able to work effectively with others in group situations.

Performance Criteria	Indicators/Evidence:
Student organizes and delegates or accepts tasks for timely completion	Percentage of assigned tasks completed on time
Student negotiates effectively in difficult situations	Faculty, peer ratings of negotiation attempts (with narrative examples)
	Group members' ratings of satisfaction with individual's contributions to negotiations
Student influences and motivates others	Voluntary involvement of others in task completion
Student interacts effectively with culturally and intellectually diverse people	Observer ratings of student's efforts to ensure equal inclusion of all participants
	Sociogram to summarize participant interaction patterns
	Participant satisfaction with interaction is equally high for majority and minority members of the group
	Inclusiveness in analysis of situations involving cultural and/or intellectual diversity

TABLE 9.6
MEASUREMENT PLAN FOR INTERPERSONAL SKILL
GOAL: CONFLICT RESOLUTION[a]

Objective: Students will be able to analyze professional situations involving conflict and offer appropriate solutions.

Performance Criteria	Indicators/Evidence:
Student clearly identifies issues and interests involved in the conflict	Analysis: Faculty ratings of student's written analysis of group situations involving interpersonal conflict
Student offers practical solutions	Performance: Peer and/or faculty ratings on checklist based on performance criteria (with narrative examples to support ratings)
Student shows clearly how proposed solution will positively affect work in the company	
Student's suggestions facilitate reduction rather than escalation of conflict	

[a]Adapted from BYU Core, Vol. II, p. 48.

TABLE 9.7
MEASUREMENT PLAN FOR GOAL:
AN ATTITUDE OF CONTINUAL INQUIRY AND LIFE-LONG LEARNING

Objective: Students will appreciate the importance of professional involvement.

Performance Criteria	Indicators/Evidence:
Student voluntarily engages in one or more of the following activities (choosing freely):	Observed or self-reported student participation rates under conditions of voluntary involvement (i.e., no program requirement specifies involvement in any of the activities listed)
• joins student chapters of professional organizations	
• attends professional meetings	
• participates in faculty research	
• completes internships in professional accounting firms	
• engages in professionally-related community service	
Student voluntarily reports plans to (affirming publicly):	
• pursue further education after graduation	
• join professional organizations after graduation	
• engage in professionally-related community service after graduation	

TABLE 9.8
ASSESSING LEARNING-TO-LEARN SKILLS

OBJECTIVE	PERFORMANCE CRITERIA	MEASUREMENT INDICATORS	MEASUREMENT STRATEGIES
Questioning: Students actively and effectively use questions to advance their understanding of a subject	Students' questions require analysis, synthesis, application, integration, or evaluation of knowledge	Cognitive complexity of students' questions based on levels of Bloom's taxonomy or "levels-of-processing" theory	Rate students' questions in class discussion Rate questions submitted by students in preparation for a major project
Organizing: Students effectively organize information for storage (retention) and subsequent retrieval	Students' organizing strategies accurately represent relationships among concepts. Students use a variety of organizing strategies for different purposes.	Appropriateness and variety in students' use of organizing strategies (outlines, matrices, flow charts, diagrams, charts, graphs, etc.)	Rate organizational strategies in students' oral and written presentations
Connecting: Students actively link new concepts and principles to prior learning and experience	Students identify linkages that accurately reflect concepts and advance understanding of accounting situations	Ratings of quality, fluency and appropriateness of linkages between concepts and prior learning or experiences	Rate key-word lists, concept maps, responses on paired concepts tests (quality of relationships identified for a given pair of terms or phrases)
Reflecting: Students reflect on what they have learned and on their own learning processes	Students demonstrate ability to extract lessons from experiences and to describe their own learning processes	Ratings of quality and appropriateness of reflective observations	Rate debriefing summaries from case discussions and simulations; rate comments in learning journals or self-assessments of strengths and weaknesses in performance on major projects
Adapting: Students use what they have learned to create new solutions to unstructured problems	Knowledge base is accurate and appropriate; solution proposals are plausible and inventive	Ratings of accuracy and appropriateness of knowledge application; ratings of solution effectiveness and inventiveness	Rate solutions to unstructured case studies, responses in simulations, project proposals, etc.

CHAPTER 10

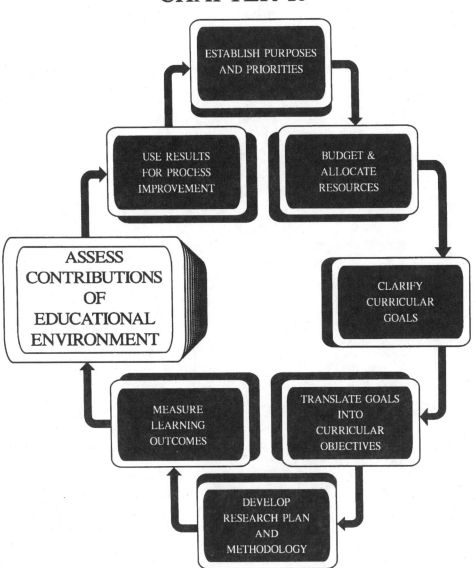

ESTABLISH PURPOSES
AND PRIORITIES

USE RESULTS
FOR PROCESS
IMPROVEMENT

BUDGET &
ALLOCATE
RESOURCES

ASSESS
CONTRIBUTIONS
OF
EDUCATIONAL
ENVIRONMENT

CLARIFY
CURRICULAR
GOALS

MEASURE
LEARNING
OUTCOMES

TRANSLATE GOALS
INTO
CURRICULAR
OBJECTIVES

DEVELOP
RESEARCH PLAN
AND
METHODOLOGY

Chapter 10
ASSESSING CONTRIBUTIONS OF THE EDUCATIONAL ENVIRONMENT

The educational environment includes all the academic influences to which students are exposed. Its assessment, therefore, is essential to understanding observed learning outcomes and planning program improvements.

This section describes assessment of the educational environment from four perspectives:

- *Curricular requirements:* to document that the means for attainment of curricular goals exist
- *Instructional emphasis:* to determine whether pedagogical practices support attainment of curricular goals
- *Student involvement:* to determine the contributions to learning outcomes of students' participation in opportunities afforded by the program
- *Stakeholders' perceptions of the program:* to determine how students, alumni, faculty, employers, and other stakeholders perceive the program and its graduates, and how they think the program can be improved

Figure 10.1 illustrates each of these perspectives.

10.1 Curricular Requirements

When the educational environment and curricular objectives are synchronized, the probability that students will achieve the goals is naturally increased. Conversely, students will have little chance of acquiring knowledge, skills, and professional orientations not emphasized in the curriculum. A review of curricular and instructional requirements enables the faculty to determine whether program goals receive adequate content and methodology attention.

A review of the curriculum can determine whether the *means* exist within the educational environment for qualified students to achieve the goals of the curriculum. The existence of requirements, however, leaves unanswered the question of whether the goals have in fact been achieved.

A straightforward way to analyze the curriculum is to review curricular requirements set forth in program documents (bulletin, advising materials, etc.). Questions such as the following should guide the review:

- Do the formal requirements of the curriculum reflect a balanced emphasis on program goals and objectives?
- Are learning-to-learn goals formally stated, recognized, and represented as part of the curriculum?
- Do the requirements ensure that students have achieved the desired level of competence (for example, achieving a certain level of performance in a course or on a proficiency examination)?

FIGURE 10.1
ASSESSING CONTRIBUTIONS OF THE EDUCATIONAL ENVIRONMENT

Curricular Requirements:
- *Review of curricular requirements:* Does the curriculum as described in program documents include requirements related to the targeted outcomes? Examples:
- Completion of a course that emphasizes the target skill
- Inclusion in the curriculum of required experiences such as writing major papers, making oral presentations, or conducting independent research
- Completion of a capstone course or project that involves a comprehensive assessment

Instructional Emphasis:
- *Analysis of syllabi and course materials:* Do course goals, assignments, examinations and projects emphasize the targeted outcomes? Criteria:
- Course activities include instruction, practice, and feedback relevant to program objectives.
- Course grades are based on performance assessments that are consistent with stated program goals.
- *Curricular Map:* A plan of goal-related activities in each course as taught by each instructor reveals good coverage and balance in use of methods to enhance students' learning-to-learn capabilities.

Student Involvement:
- *Review of transcripts*: What clusters of coursework, both in the major and the general education curriculum, contribute to student gains on analytical thinking, quantitative reasoning, communication or other valued outcomes? (Ratcliff and Jones, 1993).
- *Student self-reports:* What educational experiences do students report? How do these relate to a) self-rated progress on program objectives, and b) documented achievement on outcome measures?

Perceptions and Satisfaction:
- *Surveys, questionnaires, interviews, focus groups*: How is the program perceived by stakeholders? Examples:
  - Current Students
  - Graduating Seniors
  - Alumni
  - Recruiters
  - Employers
- *Importance/satisfaction analysis*: What priority should be assigned to improvement efforts for various aspects of the program? What strengths should be emphasized in recruitment and employer contacts?

Table 10.1 illustrates partial results of a hypothetical analysis of curricular requirements and objectives related to international accounting.

10.2 Instructional Emphasis

Complementing formal curricular requirements are the goal-related learning experiences required by faculty in their courses. Instructional emphasis can be determined by constructing a curricular map. A matrix with goals as one dimension and courses as the other uses goal-related requirements outlined in course syllabi, assignments, projects, and examinations as indicators of emphasis. Faculty then determine whether important program objectives receive balanced attention within the curriculum. Table 10.2 presents an example of a curricular map.

If the faculty believe graduates should have good writing skills, they should ensure that each semester, students complete writing instruction and assignments relevant to their future roles as professional accountants. And, are these *assignments* supported by *instruction* and *feedback* specific to the type of writing assigned? Similarly, if faculty and future employers value skill in working with diverse clients and co-workers, opportunities for interaction with a wide range of people should be *built into* the curriculum, followed by relevant feedback.

A number of instructional practices are known to be associated with desirable learning outcomes, such as increased knowledge retention and developed critical thinking skills. One important practice is the use of cooperative learning strategies, in which students work together to solve problems, study new material, or take tests. Studies in accounting and other disciplines support the use of cooperative learning (Astin, 1993; Michaelsen & others 1989; King, 1990; Bonsangue and Drew, forthcoming). Many redesigned accounting programs incorporate cooperative learning to foster skills of communication, critical thinking, and teamwork (examples include ASU, USC, and BYU; see Cottell and Millis, 1993, for examples).

Ewell has argued that the use of instructional practices known to be effective is in itself evidence of program quality (1993). However, a more persuasive approach is to include data on students' participation in such practices as part of a multivariate analysis of factors presumed to contribute to observed learning outcomes (as described below).

10.3 Student Involvement

Involvement in learning is an important predictor of student development, with some experiences more likely than others to contribute to each of the program's goals (Astin, 1993). For example, students who take courses that emphasize questioning and the application of knowledge can be expected to show greater progress on learning-to-learn measures than students who avoid such classes. Analysis of relationships between student involvement and learning outcomes, appropriately weighted for entering student characteristics, can help faculty understand patterns of progress and achievement for all students and for particular subgroups such as students of color or transfer students.

Studies that examine the relationship between student characteristics and outcomes, but fail to consider students' educational experiences, may inadvertently reinforce the status quo. For example, the authors of two recent studies using admissions data to predict students' performance in elementary and intermediate accounting find that students with higher admission test scores are more likely to do well in these courses. They conclude that admission test scores should be an important factor in student selection (Booker, 1991; Doran, Bouillon, and Smith, 1991). Neither of these studies examined the instructional methods and supports to which students were exposed, precluding the possibility of assessing whether other instructional approaches or the use of support systems might have led to enhanced success for lower-scoring students. This finding is well documented in studies of calculus instruction (e.g., Bonsangue and Drew, forthcoming), and consistent with reports of greater success rates and lower attrition in innovative accounting programs (McKenzie, p. 10; Pincus, forthcoming).

Standardized test scores may disproportionately handicap students of color, so drawing conclusions about predictors without including measures of the educational environment is risky. Moreover, since the profession seeks a stronger emphasis on producing graduates with conceptual abilities not always addressed in traditionally taught courses, studies that use performance as the dependent variable should include both a description of the instructional methods used and an analysis of the degree to which conceptual thinking is emphasized in evaluating students' performance.

Two primary sources of information on student involvement are *self-reports* and *transcripts.*

> *Self-reports* can be obtained using questionnaires on instructional practices and emphasis encountered by students in their courses as well as reports of participation in additional educational experiences such as internships, work experiences, and research with faculty. Note that self-reports (unlike perception data, described below) should not be obtained anonymously if the unit of analysis is the individual student.

> *Review of transcripts:* Transcript information can be used to identify clusters of coursework, both in the major and the general education curriculum, that appear to contribute to students' progress toward achievement of curricular objectives (Ratcliff and Jones, 1993). Transcript information can be coupled with data on instructional emphasis in particular courses for a closer analysis of factors that contribute to observed student learning outcomes.

10.4 Stakeholders' Perceptions of the Program and Program Graduates

Stakeholder feedback is an essential resource for continuous quality improvement. Students (including those who withdraw from the program), alumni, faculty, and employers or recruiters should be periodically surveyed or interviewed to determine:

- Perceptions of the program's strengths and weaknesses
- Satisfaction with various program components and the program as a whole;
- Suggestions for how the program can be improved

Students' perceptions can be assessed at strategic points in their experience, for example, when they have just completed an innovative instructional unit, upon completion of a course or coherent segment of the program, upon graduation, and after program completion when they have achieved the status of alumni. Employers and recruiters can also be surveyed at strategic moments, for example, just prior to development of a new curricular emphasis. Periodic assessment of perceptions and satisfaction is particularly important when innovations have been introduced.

> *Surveying:* At many institutions the office of institutional research administers annual surveys of current students, seniors, and alumni. These surveys typically

include questions on students' satisfaction with their majors, the advising they have received, and the faculty in their major departments, as well as questions about students' perceived progress toward achievement of curricular goals. Often a department can arrange to include additional questions for its majors and/or graduates as part of the survey effort.

Importance/Satisfaction analysis: Sifting through copious survey results is daunting without some way to identify priorities of survey respondents. A tool used in strategic marketing simplifies the task by combining data on performance and importance in a visual display of the association between these two dimensions for an array of survey items (Martilla and James, 1977). Students or other survey respondents rate each item on both dimensions, and results are plotted as shown in Figure 10.2. Areas high in importance but low in satisfaction are targets for intensive work; areas high in importance and satisfaction suggest program characteristics to emphasize in recruiting and marketing efforts.

FIGURE 10.2
IMPORTANCE/SATISFACTION ANALYSIS[3]

Extremely Important

A.
Concentrate Here

B.
Keep Up the Good Work

Very Dissatisfied   **Very Satisfied**

C.
Low Priority

D.
Possible Overkill

Slightly Important

[3]Based on Martilla and James, 1977.

A useful feature of importance/satisfaction analysis is that results can be plotted for subgroups such as transfer students, students of color, employers, and faculty. Displaying the results on transparency film, using different colors for each subgroup, allows easy identification of subgroup differences for many variables simultaneously.

Examples from accounting programs: Several accounting programs have developed surveys and interviews to assess constituents' perceptions and satisfaction. Examples include:

Survey: University of Virginia: Faculty have developed surveys for fourth-year students, alumni, and recruiters (see Appendix 10). The student and alumni surveys assess satisfaction with "personal development" in ten areas based on the AECC objectives: development of skills such as analysis, goal-setting, public speaking, writing, and problem solving and exposure to societal issues including race, gender, ethics, and international business. Surveys also assess perceived effectiveness of various instructional methods used in the McIntire School. Background information is obtained, including students' employment histories, memberships in professional societies and student social groups, GPA, and perceived impact of their interactions with faculty, students, and professionals.

Survey: BYU: At the end of the junior year, students at BYU complete an 80-question survey about all aspects of the program including teaching methods, curricular structure, learning outcomes, evaluation methods, faculty and teaching assistants (BYU Core, Vol. II, 1992, pp. 247-257). Faculty and teaching assistants are also surveyed to determine their degree of satisfaction.

Survey: Arizona State University: Faculty members administer the following open-ended questionnaire during class in the spring term:

1. What do you like about the accounting program?
2. What specific things do your professors do that are a valuable use of your time and enhance your educational experience?
3. What do you not like about the accounting program?
4. What specific things do your professors do that are not a valuable use of your time and do not enhance your educational experience?
5. Please add here any other comments you wish to make about the ASU accounting program.

Space is provided after each item to encourage written responses. The questionnaire also asks students to check which courses they have completed or are currently taking. This simple feedback mechanism provides considerable information at minimal cost.

Informal meetings: Faculty at BYU also sponsor regular, sack-lunch meetings to discuss the program (BYU Core, Vol. II, 1992). Both faculty and students participate.

TABLE 10.1

DOES THE LEARNING ENVIRONMENT SUPPORT PROGRAM GOALS?[a]

SAMPLE ANALYSIS OF CURRICULAR REQUIREMENTS

LEARNING GOAL: Students will be able to function effectively in an international business environment		LEARNING ENVIRONMENT: The program will improve students' ability to function effectively in an international business environment	
PERFORMANCE CRITERIA	EVIDENCE	PROGRAM CRITERIA: PROGRAM INCLUDES:	EVIDENCE
Student is able to: • explain and adapt to differences among major international business contexts • explain and adapt to cultural differences that may affect business transactions	Cross-grading of papers/projects dealing with international business in regular coursework Ratings of international focus in senior project Ratings of observed behavior in simulated international business situations	Required courses which contain an identifiable international business component Courses which use international business examples Assignments which require familiarity with international business problems and settings	Syllabi and course descriptions Student self-reports Course evaluations Analysis of assignments by faculty and/or practicing professionals
Student is able to: • communicate effectively in a foreign language related to their business interests	Foreign language course grades or test results	Requirement that students must be able to communicate in a major business foreign language	Documentation that foreign language study is required and completed by all students
Graduates are able to perform effectively in international business settings	Placement office inquiries Self-reports from alumni survey Employer ratings of performance	Opportunity for students to have access to faculty with international business experience or scholarly interests in international business	Number of faculty with relevant experience and/or research interest Self-reports of student contact with these faculty

[a]Adapted from a memorandum to AACSB by Peter Ewell, 1988.

TABLE 10.2
A CURRICULUM MAP

OBJECTIVE	Course						
	101	102	103	104	201	202	203
Information Function of Accounting: Role of Info Systems	X						
Concepts of System Design and Use	X						
Methods of Design and Use	X						
Application of Methods		X				X	X
Use of Technology:							
Info-gathering			X		X		
Financial data management	X		X		X	X	
Ethical Responsibilities of Accountants:							
Ethical principles	X						
Professional orientation				X		X	X
Complex Problem Solving:							
Problem-solving strategies							
Real-world applications				X		X	X
Interpersonal Skills:							
Teamwork		X		X		X	X
Negotiation			X		X	X	X
Communication Skills:							
Oral		X	X	X	X	X	X
Written	X			X	X	X	X

CHAPTER 11

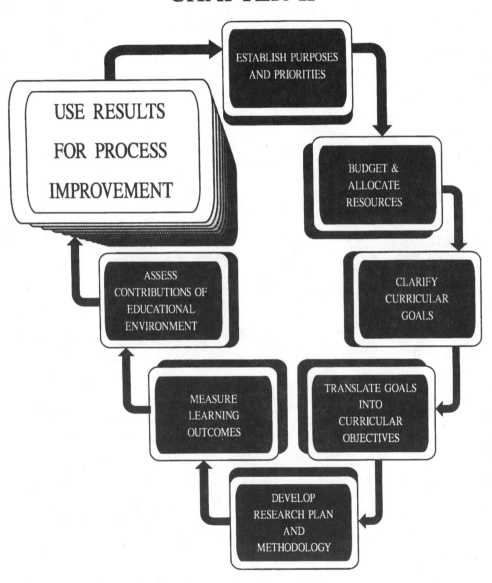

Chapter 11
USING ASSESSMENT RESULTS
FOR PROGRAM IMPROVEMENT

This brief chapter suggests approaches for reporting and using assessment results.

The plan for dissemination and use of results should specify how they will be used to achieve the purposes initially identified, for example, program planning and monitoring, curriculum improvement, resource-seeking, marketing, or public accountability. Audiences for reporting should also be identified, for example, the department chair, curriculum committee, other faculty, employers, and the general public.

11.1 Reporting Assessment Findings

Presentation of results is an important consideration in obtaining a favorable response. Assessment scholars point out that

> Within higher education, researchers must walk a fine line between turning off their audience by being too technical and turning off their audience by being too simplistic (Jacobi and others, 1987, p. 71).

Characteristics of reports that influence decision making include the following:

- Reports begin with a brief summary of the essential findings
- The questions addressed are clearly linked to real policy decisions
- At least some questions in each report consider the costs affecting policy
- Policy questions form the central organizing theme
- Evaluation methodology is played down
- Backup narrative for the executive summary is "chunked" into easily located, brief segments throughout the report
- Only simple statistics are presented
- Where jargon is used, it is the practitioners', not the evaluators'
- Concrete recommendations for action are based on *specific* findings (DeLoria and Brookins, 1984, cited in Jacobi and others, 1987, pp. 70-71)

Occasions for presentation and discussion of results should be set aside. In particular, the department chair should arrange to include results in ongoing discussions of curriculum and related issues (Jacobi, Astin, and Ayala, 1987). If the assessment has been organized around faculty needs, concerns, and questions, the results will be awaited with interest.

Presentation of numerical results can often be made more tangible by the inclusion of graphics to illustrate and vivify numerical information. Case studies and excerpted narrative comments from assessment participants will also vitalize the presentation.

11.2 Use of Results

As noted frequently in this document, the ultimate criterion for judging the success of the assessment program is whether the results are used to improve student learning. Faculty are most likely to use results if the assessment is initially designed to address problems or decisions related to students, curriculum, and/or instruction.

If faculty have been fully involved in designing and implementing the assessment program, they will be interested in the results and receptive to discussing their implications, even if changes are needed. If the program is working as it should, faculty will frequently be heard referring to assessment results, especially when making decisions about curricular and instructional issues. The faculty should be able to answer the question: How are results of assessment incorporated into the academic programs for continuous improvement?

Assessment frequently generates "fringe benefits" for the program such as improved testing, greater instructional variety, enhanced collegiality and stronger departmental focus on the curriculum. In short, it is not an end in itself but a means to an end: The enhancement of learning and the vitality of the program.

Chapter 12
IDENTIFY PROCESS IMPROVEMENTS
AND REVISE THE PLAN

The assessment plan should indicate when and how the program itself will be reviewed and judged. Questions for review are suggested by the Association of American Colleges in Figure 12.1. These questions assume assessment is an information function which enables the program to:

- Document its success
- Identify discrepancies between intended and actual outcomes
- Obtain information to guide improvements in the program
- Provide educationally valuable information to students (AAC, 1992, p. 27)

The specific purposes for which the assessment was originally designed provide a second set of criteria. The assessment program should be reviewed to determine how well those purposes have been fulfilled, where it is falling short, and what changes are needed.

Both short-term and long-term benefits and costs should affect the review process. Possible criteria include:

- Value of the process
- Impact on faculty and student vitality
- Changes in pedagogy and in-class evaluation strategies
- The degree to which assessment results facilitated improvement
- The role of assessment in generating resources for the program

In addition to questions such as those posed by the AAC (Figure 12.1), the review body should also ask pragmatic questions such as:

- Is there a better way to obtain the information we need?
- Do we need *all* the information we are collecting?
- How can we make better use of the information we have?
- Should a wider or narrower audience have access to the data?
- How can reports be made more useful?
- Whose perspectives have we overlooked in this process?
- Has the process itself enhanced collegiality, student-faculty interaction, and support for the program within the accounting community?

Program faculty and stakeholders should be actively involved in review of the assessment program. Recommendations based on the review should be implemented in a timely manner to increase the value of the assessment program as a tool for continuous improvement of quality.

FIGURE 12.1
GUIDELINES FOR REVIEW OF THE ASSESSMENT PROGRAM[4]

- What are the intended educational outcomes of the program?
  - What processes are in place for measuring the achievements of these outcomes?
  - Do the processes provide several kinds of information about student learning and achievement?
  - Do these processes reflect faculty discussion and decisions about the kinds of evidence appropriate to their program's goals, strengths, and emphases?
- Are the assessment procedures adopted by the program linked to program goals and curricular priorities?
  - Do faculty members periodically discuss the results of assessment in relation to program goals?
  - Do they use assessment evidence in making judgments about curriculum development and revisions?
- Does assessment provide opportunities for students to reflect on their progress in the program? To integrate different parts of their learning?
  - Do students who take part in assessment activities receive feedback on their performance?
  - Is there a culture that invites students to take assessment seriously as a milestone in their learning and intellectual development?
- If assessment examinations and assignments are locally developed, are faculty members given release time or other compensation to design them?
  - Who is involved in making judgments about the outcomes of assessment?
  - Who uses the results?
  - Do faculty members in the program confer with peers in comparable programs in reviewing the outcomes of assessment activities?
  - Are there opportunities for students to discuss assessment outcomes in relation to their experience in the program?
- To what extent are intended [curricular] outcomes achieved?
  - To the extent that the intellectual outcomes are not achieved, what changes are being made either in the goals of the program or in the program itself?

---

[4]AAC, 1992, pp. 27-28.

Epilogue
ACHIEVING THE PROMISE OF ASSESSMENT

Throughout this guide, practical approaches to assessment have been emphasized. Assessment need not be postponed simply because grant funds are not available or because the department has a limited budget for this purpose. Important insights can be gained for little more than the cost of duplicating and processing questionnaires or providing refreshments for a series of focus groups. Once the department begins to generate data about the program, however, the discussion inevitably raises questions worthy of further investigation. A faculty champion (or several champions) may be needed to obtain the resources to pursue these questions. The research skills and ingenuity of the faculty are important resources, but administrators must recognize that faculty energy is a finite resource. Both tangible and intangible administrative support are necessary if the "culture of evidence" is to become the standard of practice in accounting education.

GLOSSARY

Accreditation: A formal process of review and certification in which an institution's or program's status is legitimized by an external agency.

Affective objectives: Desired learning outcomes related to beliefs, attitudes, and values.

Assessment Plan: A statement of the purpose of a departmental assessment program, the curricular goals and objectives that will be assessed, the methods and measures that will be used to determine students' progress toward these goals and objectives, the estimated costs and benefits of the program, and the procedures that will be used to integrate the findings into ongoing program improvement and documentation of success.

Assessment: In education, the systematic collection, interpretation, and use of information on student characteristics, the educational environment, and learning outcomes to improve student learning and client satisfaction and/or to document program success.

Bloom's taxonomy of educational objectives: A system of categorizing cognitive outcomes of education in six levels: Knowledge, Comprehension, Application, Analysis, Synthesis, and Evaluation. Each level progressively requires greater understanding of concepts and principles and flexibility in adapting knowledge for particular purposes.

Cognitive objectives: Desired learning outcomes related to the acquisition and use of knowledge.

Criterion-referenced testing: Testing intended to determine how well students perform relative to specified objectives of a course or program.

Goals: The desired outcomes of a program. *Curricular* goals in professional education define in broad terms the knowledge, skills, values, and attitudes most valued by the faculty and which the faculty believes will enable graduates to succeed as practicing professionals.

Indicators: Forms of evidence that reasonable observers would agree attest to the attainment of a specific educational outcome.

Institutional Assessment: A comprehensive inquiry to determine the effectiveness of all aspects of an educational institution. The term "assessment" suggests an emphasis on the use of data, including data on the consequences of the institution's activities as well as its resources, the services it provides, and constituents' satisfaction.

Learning outcomes: Educational results in the domain of cognition, skills, or attitudes and values. Taxonomies of learning outcomes further subdivide these domains, for example, Bloom's taxonomy which offers six levels of cognitive outcomes (see Bloom's Taxonomy); Raths and Simon offer six levels in the affective domain (attitudes and values).

Formative evaluation: Use of evaluation methods and results for program improvement. May include evidence of students' progress toward desired outcomes of the program as well as information on students' and other stakeholders' perceptions of the program and how it can be improved.

Norm-referenced testing: Testing designed to rank-order students' performances relative to each other.

Objectives: Operationally defined statements of desired learning outcomes. Also known as "performance objectives" or "behavioral objectives" because they identify what the learner should be able to *do* as a result of participating in a particular educational experience.

Outcomes: In education, the results of an educational experience, intended or unintended. The term usually implies measurability, although the vast majority of outcomes are not measured and many do not lend themselves to measurement. Learning outcomes include knowledge, skills, and attitudes and values. Additional outcomes include the actual consequences of the experience, for example, employment, opportunities for advancement, or enhanced credibility as an authority in one's professional field.

Performance measures: Evidence of attainment of learning outcomes based on behavioral demonstration of the desired knowledge, skills, attitudes, or values.

Performance criteria: Standards by which an individual's performance on a particular task can be judged.

Program Review: A systematic and comprehensive analysis of a program's characteristics and results, often conducted with the assistance of (or at the request of) authorities external to the program, for example, institutional administrators or accrediting agencies.

Proxy indicators: Evidence used to suggest that a given educational outcome has been achieved, without directly measuring that outcome. Proxy indicators are of two types: evidence that the *means* exist to achieve the outcome, and evidence based on testimonials rather than actual performances relevant to the outcome (for example, self-reports of skill or knowledge levels)

Summative evaluation: Evaluation designed primarily to judge program achievements and to ascertain the merits of the program.

RESOURCES AND REFERENCES

AAA Committee on the Future Content, Structure and Scope of Accounting Education (The Bedford Committee). 1986 (Spring). "Future Accounting Education: Preparing for the Expanded Profession." *Issues in Accounting Education, 1* (1), 168-195.

AAHE Assessment Forum. 1992 (December). *Assessment Principles of Good Practice.* Washington, DC: American Association for Higher Education.

Accounting Education Change Commission (AECC). 1990 (September). *Position Statement No. 1: Objectives of Education for Accountants.*

Albrecht, W. S., Clark, D.C., Smith, J.M., Stocks, K.D., and Woodfield, L.W. No date. *An Accounting Curriculum for the Next Century.* Unpublished manuscript. Provo, Utah: Brigham Young University.

Anderson, J.R. 1985. *Cognitive Psychology and Its Implications.* New York, NY: W.H. Freeman.

Anderson, S., Ball, S., Murphy, R.T., and Associates. 1975. *The Encyclopedia of Educational Evaluation.* San Francisco: Jossey-Bass.

Angelo, T. (Ed.) 1991 (Summer). *Classroom Research: Early Lessons from Success.* New Directions for Teaching and Learning No. 46.

Angelo, T. H., and Cross, K.P. 1993. Classroom Assessment Techniques (2nd Edition). San Francisco: Jossey-Bass.

Arthur Andersen & Co., Arthur Young, Coopers & Lybrand, Deloitte Haskins & Sells, Ernst & Whinney, Peat Marwick Main & Co., Price Waterhouse, and Touche Ross. 1989 (April). *Perspectives on Education: Capabilities for Success in the Accounting Profession.* New York: Authors.

Association of American Colleges (AAC). 1992. *Program Review and Educational Quality in the Major: A Faculty Handbook.* Washington, DC: AAC.

Astin, A.W. 1985. *Achieving Educational Excellence.* San Francisco: Jossey-Bass.

Astin, A.W. 1993. *What Matters in College? Four Critical Years Revisited.* San Francisco: Jossey-Bass.

Baker, R., Bayer, F., Gabbin, A., Izard, D., Jacobs, F., and Polejewski, S. 1993. *Report of the 1992-93 Outcomes Assessment Committee.* American Accounting Association, Teaching and Curricula Section.

Ball State University. No date. *Assessment Workbook.* Offices of Academic Assessment & Institutional Research.

Banta, Trudy. 1985. Use of Outcomes Information at the University of Tennessee, Knoxville. In *Assessing Educational Outcomes,* edited by Peter Ewell. New Directions for Institutional Research, No. 47. San Francisco: Jossey-Bass.

Banta, T.W., and Schneider, J.A. 1988 (January/February). Using Faculty-Developed Exit Examinations to Evaluate Academic Programs. *Journal of Higher Education,* Vol. 59, No. 1, pp. 69-83.

Banta, T.W. and associates. 1993. *Making a Difference: Outcomes of a Decade of Assessment in Higher Education.* San Francisco: Jossey-Bass.

Bayer, F.A. 1993 (December). Measuring Students' Development of Communication Skills. Presentation at the Seventeenth Annual Meeting of the Federation of Schools of Accountancy. Tampa, Florida.

Bayer, Frieda A. 1993 (August). Preliminary results, Survey of Assessment Programs in Accounting Education, Federation of Schools of Accountancy. Personal communication.

Bayer, F.A., Clark, D.C., Herring, H.C. III, and Thomas, L.R. 1992 (October). Evaluating Your Curriculum: Initial Concepts to Consider. Unpublished paper.

Bayer, F.A., Luker, W.A., Michaelsen, R.H., and Wilner, N. 1993 (January). A Cross-sectional Regression Analysis of Career-relevant Skills among Students at Different Stages in an Accounting Program. Unpublished manuscript, University of North Texas.

Belanoff, P., and Elbow, P. 1986. Using Portfolios to Increase Collaboration and Community in a Writing Program. *Writing Program Administration*, Vol. 9, No. 3, 27-40.

Bloom, Benjamin S. (Ed.) 1956. *Taxonomy of Educational Objectives: The Classification of Educational Goals, by a Committee of College and University Examiners.* Handbook I. Cognitive Domain. New York: Longmans, Green.

Bonner, S.E., and Walker, P.L. 1994. The Effects of Instruction and Experience on the Acquisition of Auditing Knowledge. *The Accounting Review,* Vol. 69, No. 1, 157-178.

Bonsangue, M.V., and Drew, D.E. (forthcoming). Increasing Minority Students' Success in Calculus. In J. Gainen and E. Willemsen (eds.) *Fostering Success in Quantitative Gateway Courses.* New Directions for Teaching and Learning. San Francisco: Jossey-Bass.

Booker, Quinton. 1991 (Spring). A Case Study of the Relationship between Undergraduate Black Accounting Majors' ACT Scores and their Intermediate Accounting Performance. *Issues in Accounting Education, 6* (1), 66-73.

Boyer, E.L. 1990. *Scholarship Reconsidered: Priorities of the Professoriate.* Princeton, NJ: The Carnegie Foundation for the Advancement of Teaching.

Brigham Young University Integrated Jr. Year Core Faculty 1990-92 Implementation Team (BYU Core). 1992. *Report to AECC. Volumes I and II.* Provo, Utah: Brigham Young University.

Campbell, D.T., and Stanley, J.C. 1966. *Experimental and Quasi-Experimental Designs for Research.* Chicago: Rand McNally.

Carpenter, V.L., Friar, S., and Lipe, M.G. 1993. Evidence on the Performance of Accounting Students: Race, Gender, and Expectations. *Issues in Accounting Education, 8* (1), 1-17.

Center for Faculty Evaluation and Development. 1975. *Development of the IDEA System.* IDEA Technical Report No. 1. Manhattan, KS: Kansas State University.

Chamberlain, D., Seay, R., and Julian, F. 1991 (Winter). Accounting Administrators' Perceptions of the Status and Usefulness of Outcome Measurement. *The Accounting Educators' Journal,* pp. 18-29.

Conry, E.J., and D.R. Nelson, 1989 (Spring). Business Law and Moral Growth. *American Business Law Journal, 27,* No. 1, pp. 1-39.

Cottell, P., Jr., and Millis, Barbara. 1993 (Spring). Cooperative Learning Structures in the Instruction of Accounting. *Issues in Accounting Education, 8* (1), 40-59.

Davis, B.G. 1989 (Fall). Demystifying Assessment: Learning from the Field of Evaluation. In *Achieving Assessment Goals Using Evaluation Techniques*, edited by Peter J. Gray. New Directions for Higher Education No. 67, pp. 5-20.

DeLoria, D., and Brookins, G.K. 1984. The Evaluation Report: A Weak Link to Policy. In *Evaluation Studies Review Annual Volume 9*, edited by Ross Conner. Beverly Hills, CA: Sage Publishers.

DeMong, R.F., Lindgren, J.H., Jr., and Perry, S.E. 1994 (Spring). Designing an Assessment Program for Accounting. *Issues in Accounting Education, (9)* 1, 11-27.

Deppe, L.A., Sonderegger, E.O., Stice, J.D., Clark, D.C., and Streuling, G.F. 1991. Emerging Competencies for the Practice of Accountancy. *Journal of Accounting Education, 9,* 257-290.

Diamond, Michael A., and Pincus, Karen V. 1994. *The USC Year 2000 Curriculum Project.* New York: Coopers & Lybrand Foundation.

Dirsmith, M., and Ketz, J.E. 1987. A Fifty-cent Test: An Approach to Teaching Integrity. *Advances in Accounting, 4,* 129-141.

Domino, G. 1971. Interactive Effects of Achievement Orientation and Teaching style on Academic Achievement. *Journal of Educational Psychology, 62,* 427-431.

Doran, M.B., Bouillon, M.J., and Smith, C.G. 1991 (Spring). Determinants of Student Performance in Accounting Principles I and II. *Issues in Accounting Education, 6* (1), 74-84.

El-Khawas, E. 1990 (July). *Campus Trends, 1990* Higher Education Panel Report No. 80. Washington, D.C.: American Council on Education.

Elliott, R.K. 1991 (Spring). Accounting Education and Research at the Crossroad. *Issues in Accounting Education, 6* (1), 1-8.

Erwin, T.D. 1991. *Assessing Student Learning and Development: A Guide to the Principles, Goals, and Methods of Determining College Outcomes.* San Francisco: Jossey-Bass.

Ewell, P. 1992. Outcomes Assessment, Institutional Effectiveness, and Accreditation: A Conceptual Exploration. In *Accreditation, Assessment, and Institutional Effectiveness.* Washington, DC: Council on Postsecondary Education.

Ewell, P.T. (Ed.) 1985 (September). *Assessing Educational Outcomes.* New Directions for Institutional Research No. 47. San Francisco: Jossey-Bass.

Ewell, P.T. 1988. Memorandum to AACSB on assessment.

Ewell, P.T. 1991a (November/December). Assessment and Public Accountability: Back to the Future. *Change,* 12-17.

Ewell, P,T. 1991b. To Capture the Ineffable: New Forms of Assessment in Higher Education. In Grant, G. (ed.) *Review of Research in Education, 17,* 75-125.

Ewell, P.T. 1993 (September). *A Preliminary Study of the Feasibility and Utility for National Policy of Instructional 'Good Practice' Indicators in Undergraduate Education.* Boulder, CO: National Center for Education Management Systems.

Ewell, P.T. 1994. *A Policy Guide for Assessment: Making Good Use of Tasks of Critical Thinking.* Educational Testing Service.

Facione, P.A. 1990a. *The California Critical Thinking Skills Test: College Level.* Millbrae, CA.: California Academic Press.

Facione, P.A. 1990b. *The California Critical Thinking Skills Test: College Level. Technical Report #2—Factors Predictive of CT Skills.* Millbrae, CA.: California Academic Press.

Facione, P.A., Sanchez, C., Facione, N., and Gainen, J., forthcoming. The Disposition Toward Critical Thinking, *Journal of General Education.*

Farmer, D. 1988. *Enhancing Student Learning: Emphasizing Essential Competencies in Academic Programs.* Wilkes-Barre, PA: Kings College.

Federation of Schools of Accountancy (FSA). In preparation. Task Force on Assessment.

Ferris, K. 1982. Educational Predictors of Professional Pay and Performance. *Accounting, Organizations, and Society, 1* (3), 225-230.

Finn and others. 1988. Ethical Problems in Public Accounting: The View from the Top, *Journal of Business Ethics, 7,* 605-615.

Fisher, R., Ury, W., and Patton, B. 1991. *Getting to Yes: Negotiating Agreement Without Giving In* (second edition). New York: Penguin Books.

Francis, M.C., Mulder, T.C., and Stark, J.S. forthcoming. *Intentional Learning: A Process for Learning to Learn in the Accounting Curriculum.* Accounting Education Change Commission and American Accounting Association.

Frank, B.M. 1984 (Fall). Effect of Field Independence-Dependence and Study Technique on Learning from a Lecture. *American Educational Research Journal, 21* (3), 669-678.

Fuhrmann, B. S., and Grasha, A.F., 1982. *A Practical Handbook for College Teachers.* Boston, MA: Little, Brown and Company.

Gabriel, S. L., and Hirsch, M.L., Jr. 1992. Critical Thinking and Communication Skills: Integration and Implementation Issues. *Journal of Accounting Education, 10,* 243-270.

Gardiner, L. F. 1989. *Planning for Assessment: Mission Statements, Goals, and Objectives.* Trenton, N.J.: New Jersey Department of Higher Education, Office of Learning Assessment.

Geary, W.T., and Rooney, C.J. 1993 (Spring). Designing Accounting Education to Achieve Balanced Intellectual Development. *Issues in Accounting Education, 8* (1), 60-70.

Glaser, R. 1984. Education and Thinking: The Role of Knowledge. *American Psychologist, 13* (9), 5-10.

Gray, P.J., Editor. 1989 (Fall) *Achieving Assessment Goals Using Evaluation Techniques.* New Directions for Higher Education No. 67. San Francisco: Jossey-Bass.

Greenberg, K.L. 1988 (Summer). Assessing Writing: Theory and Practice. In J.H. McMillan (ed.), *Assessing Students' Learning.* New Directions for Teaching and Learning No. 34.

Greenberg, S., and Smith, I.L. 1991. *Practice Analysis of Certified Public Accountants in Public Accounting.* New York, NY: AICPA.

Heffernan, J.M., Hutchings, P., and Marchese, T.J. No date. *Standardized Tests and the Purposes of Assessment.* Washington, DC: American Association for Higher Education Assessment Forum.

Herring, H.C. III, and Izard, D. 1992 (Spring). Outcomes Assessment of Accounting Majors. *Issues in Accounting Education, 7* (1), 1-17.

Hiltebeitel, K.M. and Jones, S.K. 1991 (Fall). Initial Evidence on the Impact of Integrating Ethics into Accounting Education. *Issues in Accounting Education, 6* (2), 262-275.

Ingram, R.W., and Petersen, R.J. 1987. An Evaluation of AICPA Tests for Predicting the Performance of Accounting Majors. *The Accounting Review, 62,* 215-223.

Inman, B.C., Wenzler, A., and Wickert, P.D. 1989. Square Pegs in Round Holes: Are Accounting Students Well-suited to Today's Accounting Profession? *Issues in Accounting Education, 4* (1), 29-47.

Jacobi, M.; Astin, A.; and Ayala, F., Jr. *College Student Outcomes Assessment: A Talent Development Perspective.* ASHE-ERIC Higher Education Reports No. 7, 1987. Washington, DC: Association for the Study of Higher Education-ERIC.

Jeffrey, C. 1993 (Spring), Ethical Development of Accounting Students, Non-Accounting Business Students, and Liberal Arts Students. *Issues in Accounting Education, 8* (1), 86-96.

Johnson, D. W., Johnson, R.T., and Smith, K. A. 1991. *Cooperative Learning: Increasing College Faculty Instructional Productivity.* ASHE-ERIC Higher Education Report No. 4. Washington, D.C.: Association for the Study of Higher Education.

Johnson, Reid. 1993. Assessment Options for the College Major. In Banta, T.W. and associates. 1993. *Making a Difference: Outcomes of a Decade of Assessment in Higher Education.* San Francisco: Jossey-Bass.

Joint Committee on Standards for Educational Evaluation. 1981. Proprietary Standards. *Standards for Evaluation of Educational Programs, Projects and Materials.* New York: McGraw-Hill.

King, A. 1990 (Winter). Enhancing Peer Interaction and Learning in the Classroom through Reciprocal Questioning. *American Educational Research Journal, 27* (4), 664-687.

Kitchener, K.S. 1990. Assessing Reflective Thinking within Curricular Contexts. In FIPSE Program Book. Washington, D.C.

Kohlberg, L. 1976. Moral Stages and Moralization: The Cognitive Developmental Approach. In *Moral Development and Behavior: Theory, Research, and Social Issues.* T. Lickona (ed.). New York: Holt, Rinehart, and Winston.

KPMG Peat Marwick. 1993 (September). *Developing a Report Card: A Summary of Research and Practices.* New York: KPMG Peat Marwick and New York City public schools. Draft report.

Kraemer, H.C., and Thiemann, S. 1987. *How Many Subjects? Statistical Power Analysis in Research.* Beverly Hills: Sage Publications.

Krathwohl, D., Bloom, B.S., and Massia, B.B. 1964. *Taxonomy of Educational Objectives, Handbook II: Affective Domain.* New York: David McKay Company, Inc.

Kurfiss, J.G. 1988. *Critical Thinking: Theory, Research, Practice and Possibilities.* ASHE-ERIC Higher Education Report No. 2. Washington, D.C.: Association for the Study of Higher Education.

Libby, Patricia A. 1991. Barriers to Using Cases in Accounting Education. *Issues in Accounting Education,* 6 (2), 193-213.

Light, R.J., Singer, J.D., and Willet, J.B. 1990. *By Design: Planning Research on Higher Education.* Cambridge, MA: Harvard University Press.

Loacker, G., Cromwell, L., Fey, J., and Rutherford, D. 1984. *Analysis and Communication at Alverno: An Approach to Critical Thinking.* Milwaukee, WI: Alverno Productions.

Loacker, G.; Cromwell, L.; and O'Brien, K. 1986. Assessment in Higher Education: To Serve the Learner. In *Assessment in Higher Education: Issues and Contexts,* C. Adelman, editor. Washington, D. C.: Office of Educational Research and Improvement, U. S. Department of Education, 47-61.

MacCrate, R. (Ed.), 1992. *Legal Education and Professional Development—An Educational Continuum.* Student edition. American Bar Association,

Marsh, H.W. 1980. The Influence of Student, Course, and Instructor Characteristics in Evaluations of University Teaching. *American Educational Research Journal, 17* (1), 219-237.

Martilla, J.A., and James, J.C. 1977 (January). Importance-Performance Analysis. *Journal of Marketing,* 77-79.

McBeath, R.J. (Ed.). 1992. *Instructing and Evaluating in Higher Education: A Guidebook for Planning Learning Outcomes.* Englewood Cliffs, NJ: Educational Technology Publications.

McKenzie, P. Project Description in Williams, D.Z. and Gary L. Sundem. 1991. AECC Additional Grants Awarded for Implementation of Improvements in Accounting Education. *Issues in Accounting Education,* 6 (2), 315-330.

McMillan, J.H. 1987. Enhancing College Students' Critical Thinking: A Review of Studies. *Research in Higher Education, 26* (1), 3-29.

McMillan, J.H. 1988 (Summer). *Assessing Students' Learning.* New Directions for Teaching and Learning No. 34.

McPeck, J. 1981. *Critial Thinking and Education.* New York: St. Martin's Press.

Metfessel, Michael, and Kirsner. 1967. Instrumentation of Bloom's and Krathwohl's Taxonomies for the Writing of Educational Objectives. *Psychology in Schools, 27*, 228-229.

Michaelsen, L.K., Watson, W.E., and Black, R.H. 1989. A Realistic Test of Individual versus Group Consensus Decision Making. *Journal of Applied Psychology, 74* (5), 834-839.

Mohrweis, Lawrence C. 1993 (Fall). Teaching Audit Planning and Risk Assessment: An Empirical Test of the Dermaceutics Instructional Resources. *Issues in Accounting Education, 8* (2), 391-403.

Moore, Wm. 1987. *Learning Environment Preferences (LEP)*. Olympia, WA: Center for the Study of Intellectual Development.

National Council of Teachers of Mathematics. 1993. *Assessment Standards for School Mathematics*, Working Draft. Reston, VA.: NCTM.

Nelson, I.T. 1992. *Identification and Recruitment of Future Professionals: An Empirical Study of Highly Capable Individuals' Attitudes toward the Accounting Profession.* Unpublished Dissertation, Univ. of Nebraska.

Ott, R.L., Mann, M.H., and Moores, C.T. An Empirical Investigation into the Interactive Effects of Student Personality Traits and Method of Instruction (Lecture or CAI) on Student Performance in Elementary Accounting. *Journal of Accounting Education*, 1990, Vol. 8, pp. 17-35.

Pascarella, E. T., and Terenzini, P.T. 1991. *How College Affects Students*. San Francisco: Jossey-Bass.

Peterson, P.L. 1979. Aptitude X Treatment Interaction Effects of Teacher Structuring and Student Participation in College Instruction. *Journal of Educational Psychology, 71* (4).

Pincus, K.V. 1993. *Core Concepts of Accounting Information: Planning Guide for Course Instructors.* New York, McGraw-Hill.

Pincus, K.V. (forthcoming). Introductory Accounting: Changing the First Course. In J. Gainen and E. Willemsen (eds). *Fostering Success in Quantitative Gateway Courses.* New Directions for Teaching and Learning. San Francisco: Jossey-Bass.

Pincus, K., Scott, L., Searfoss, J., and Clark, C. 1993 (August). Transitioning for Change: Summary of Interview Data from Twelve Schools. Unpublished document distributed at meeting of the AECC Grant Schools.

Ponemon, L.A. 1993. Can Ethics be Taught in Accounting? *Journal of Accounting Education, 11*, 185-209.

Ratcliff, J.L., and Jones, E.A. 1993. Coursework Cluster Analysis, in Banta and associates, 1993. *Making a Difference: Outcomes of a Decade of Assessment in Higher Education.* San Francisco: Jossey-Bass.

Raths, L., Harmin, M., and Simon, S. 1966. *Values and Teaching.* Columbus, Ohio: Charles E. Merrill.

Rebele, J.E., Stout, D.E., and Hassell, J.M. 1991. A Review of Empirical Research in Accounting Education: 1985-1991. *Journal of Accounting Education, 9*, 167-231.

Rest, J.R. 1990. *Defining Issues Test Manual.* Minneapolis, MN: University of Minnesota.

Rest, J. 1986. *Moral Development: Advances in Research and Theory.* New York, NY: Praeger.

Romberg, E. (Ed.) 1990. *Outcomes Assessment: A Resource Book.* American Association of Dental Schools Special Committee on Outcomes Assessment.

Scofield, B. 1994 (November). Oral Communication Skills in the Accounting Classroom. Presentation at the 1994 Accounting Educator's Mini-conference, Portland, OR.

Scofield, B., and Combes, L. 1993. Designing and Managing Meaningful Writing Assignments. *Issues in Accounting Education, 8* (1), 71-85.

Schroeder, C.C. 1993 (September/October). New Students—New Learning Styles. *Change*, 21-26.

Smith, M. K., Draper, G. F., and Bradley, J. L. 1994. *Annotated Reference Catalog of Assessment Instruments in the Major: Business and Communications (Catalog E2)*. Knoxville, TN.: University of Tennessee Clearinghouse.

Snow, R.E., and Peterson, P.L. 1980. Recognizing Differences in Student Aptitudes. In *Learning, Cognition and College Teaching*. W.J. McKeachie (Ed.). New Directions for Teaching and Learning No. 2, 1-24.

St. Pierre, E.K., Nelson, E.S., and Gabbin, A.L. 1990 (Summer). A Study of the Ethical Development of Accounting Majors in Relation to Other Business and Nonbusiness Disciplines. *The Accounting Educators' Journal*, 23-35.

Terenzini, P.T. 1989 (November/December). Assessment with Open Eyes: Pitfalls in Studying Student Outcomes. *Journal of Higher Education, 60* (6), 645-664.

Velasquez, Manny G. 1992. *Business Ethics: Concepts and Cases*. Englewood Cliffs, NJ: Prentice-Hall (Third edition).

Ward, S.P., Ward, D.R., Wilson, T.E., Jr., and Deck, A.B. 1993. Further Evidence on the Relationship Between ACT Scores and Accounting Performance of Black Students. *Issues in Accounting Education, 8* (2), 239-247.

White, E. 1985. *Teaching and Assessing Writing: Recent Advances in Understanding, Evaluating, and Improving Student Performance*. San Francisco: Jossey-Bass.

Williams, J.R., Tiller, M.G., Herring, H.C., III, and Scheiner, J. 1988. *A Framework for the Development of Accounting Education Research*. Sarasota, FL: Coopers and Lybrand Foundation and American Accounting Association.

Wolff, R.A. 1990 (June). Assessment and Accreditation: A Shotgun Marriage? Paper presented at the AAHE Conference on Assessment in Higher Education. Washington, DC: AAHE.

Wolff, R.A., and Harris, O.D. 1994. Using Assessment to Develop a Culture of Evidence. In D. Halpern (Ed.). *Changing College Classrooms*. San Francisco: Jossey-Bass.

Wyer, J.C. 1984. Procedural v. Conceptual: A Developmental View. *Journal of Accounting Education, 2* (1), 5-18.

Wyer, J.C. 1992. Sources and Resources in Teaching and Learning. In T.J. Frecka (Ed.), *Critical Thinking, Interactive Learning and Technology: Reaching for Excellence in Business Education*. Arthur Andersen and Co.

APPENDIX 1
STUDENTS' SELF-RATED KNOWLEDGE
OF AUDIT PLANNING AND RISK ASSESSMENT[a]

Students were asked to rate their knowledge of the following topics using a 7-point scale from 1 = minimal knowledge to 7 = high level of knowledge.

1. Audit planning process, including assessing risk and making preliminary materiality judgments.

2. Importance of the auditor's understanding of the client's business and industry.

3. Auditor's exercise of judgment in the conduct of the audit.

4. Need for flexibility in the design and revision of the audit strategy.

5. Necessity for the audit strategy to be responsive to inherent and control risks.

6. Interaction of auditors with the client.

7. Need for professionalism in conducting an audit.

8. Business aspects of auditing, requiring attention to audit risk and the public interest.

9. Perception of auditing as an exciting and challenging career.

---

[a]Mohrweis, 1993, p. 399.

APPENDIX 2
SURVEY OF ACCOUNTING STUDENT CHARACTERISTICS

School of Accountancy
Supplemental Learning Assessment

Please indicate (mark with a No. 2 pencil) the best answer for each of the following on the separate answer sheet.

Part I: Background
1. Please indicate your academic status:
   A = Freshman,   B = Sophomore, C = Junior,   D = Senior,   E = Graduate

2. Please indicate your gender:
   A = Female,   B = Male

3. Your racial/ethnic background (voluntary):
   A = Asian,   B = Black,   C = Hispanic,   D = White (non-Hispanic)
   E = Other

4. Your college GPA at the start of this semester was:
   A = 2.0 or less,   B = 2.01 to 2.50, C = 2.51 to 3.0, D = 3.01 to 3.5, E = 3.51 to 4.0

Part II: Your progress in learning Accounting-related Skills and Abilities

*Use the following scale, please indicate the extent that you **agree or disagree** with the following:*

Strongly Agree	Tend To Agree	Neither Agree nor Disagree	Tend To Disagree	Strongly Disagree
A	B	C	D	E

During this course, I have improved my skill or ability to ...

5. Learn on my own and make learning a lifelong habit (improved learning skills).

6. Write and speak proficiently and effectively (improved communication skills).

7. Think critically and reason logically in both structured and unstructured decision situations (improved decision-making skills).

8. Understand the needs of managers and entrepreneurs, and create new ideas, develop strategies and innovative solutions (improve problem solving skills).

9. To effectively work with others and relate positively with others from different backgrounds (improve interpersonal skills).

10. Develop a reasoned decision in situations of ethical dilemma and an awareness of the need to maintain high standards of professional ethics (improve ethical skills).

Part III: Effectiveness of Cooperative Learning (CL)
Cooperative Learning is an active learning strategy (an alternative to the traditional lecture method) which utilizes structured group assignments to develop positive interdependence, face-to-face promotive interaction, individual accountability, interpersonal and small group skills, and improved group processing.

11. Please indicate the number of courses you have taken in which Cooperative Learning was the primary instructional method.
    A = None   B = One   C = Two   D = Three   E = Four or more

12. Please estimate the percentage of class time spent on Cooperative Learning activities in this class.
    A = None   B = 1 to 25%   C = 26 to 50%   D = 51 to 75%   E = 76 to 100%

*Using the following scale, please compare the **effectiveness** of Cooperative Learning in this class with the traditional forms of college instruction (e.g. lecture method) for each of the following objectives:*

Significantly More Effective	Somewhat More Effective	Equally Effective	Somewhat Less Effective	Significantly Less Effective
A	B	C	D	E

13. Promoting general academic interest.
14. Developing higher level thinking skills.
15. Creating interest in the subject matter.
16. Increasing likelihood of attending class.
17. Increasing frequency and quality of contact with instructor.
18. Increasing percent of time I paid attention in class.
19. Increasing my ability to diagnose my own knowledge of subject matter.
20. Increasing the frequency and quality of interactions with classmates.
21. Reducing the amount of class time needed to learn a concept.
22. Improving class morale.
23. Promoting rapport with instructor.
24. Overall evaluation of cooperative learning in this class.

Part IV: Instructional Objectives: Pre and Post Course Skills and Abilities

Using the following scale, please indicate your level of skill (ability to perform) prior to the (PRE) and after this course (POST):

Very High A	High B	Neither High Nor Low C	Low D	Very Low E

Ability to read, understand, and apply technical knowledge.
25. PRE, Prior to this course.
26. POST, After this course.

Ability to use interpersonal skills and group problem solving skills (abilities) to resolve technical and non technical issues and reach a group decision.
27. PRE, Prior to this course.
28. POST, After this course.

Ability to analyze, synthesize, and evaluate technical issues.
29. PRE, Prior to this course.
30. POST, After this course.

Ability to research and analyze a technical issue, and to write a memo/letter effectively communicating findings to a nontechnical reader.
31. PRE, Prior to this course.
32. POST, After this course.

Ability to make an effective presentation to a large audience.
33. PRE, Prior to this course.
34. POST, After this course.

Ability to recognize ethical dilemmas and evaluate alternative responses.
35. PRE, Prior to this course.
36. POST, After this course.

Ability to utilize computer (information technology) resources to obtain and analyze information or data necessary to evaluate/solve a technical issue or problem.
37. PRE, Prior to this course.
38. POST, After this course.

Part V: Comments

We are particularly interested in your comments and impressions of the Cooperative Learning process and the laboratory course format. Your candid comments will help us improve the program and this evaluation process.

A. Describe three problems or weaknesses you observed in Cooperative Learning activities in this class.

1.

2.

3.

B. Describe three positive experiences you observed in Cooperative Learning activities in this class.

1.

2.

3.

C. The three hour per week laboratory period was added to this course to facilitate a variety of learning objectives. Please describe three examples or instances in which the laboratory experience enhanced your learning process or in some way was a positive value added experience.

1.

2.

3.

D. The three hour per week laboratory period was added to this course to facilitate a variety of learning objectives. Please describe three examples or incidents in which the laboratory experience detracted from your learning experience or in other ways was not a value added experience.

1.

2.

3.

Thank you for your comments.

APPENDIX 3
ANALYTIC CRITERIA FOR EVALUATING CONTENT AND PROCESS
IN A WRITING ASSIGNMENT[a]

Process-Oriented Writing Assignment

PROFESSIONAL REPORT #3

Topic:	Pronouncements
Writer:	Controller for a small, privately held corporation at the end of its first year of operation
Audience:	Chief Executive Officer of the corporation
Report Type:	Intracompany memorandum
Length of Report:	2-5 pages with an appendix of two balance sheets
Credit:	40 points

Your CEO has asked you to draft the balance sheet for the company. Since you know that the same information can be communicated in several different ways and you are unsure which will be preferred by the CEO, you prepare two alternative balance sheets for the CEO and indicate in your memorandum your recommendation based on your knowledge of authoritative pronouncements (cite specifically both GAAP and SEC), accounting theory and the potential business consequences of different financial statement presentations.

Grading Criteria for Students

PROFESSIONAL REPORTING GRADE SHEET: PROFESSIONAL REPORT #3

Name: _____Grade: _____

CONTENT (75 points = 75%)
_____   10 Cites appropriate SEC pronouncements
_____   10 Cites appropriate FASB pronouncements
_____   15 Classified balance sheets in accordance with GAAP and at least 1 in accordance with SEC
_____   40 Provides comprehensive, insightful and logical support for balance sheet recommended. Demonstrates an understanding of accounting policy choice.

*   *   *   *   *   *   *   *   *   *   *

WRITING (25 points = 25%)
_____   5 Writes in a concise, professional tone of an expert controller to a nonexpert CEO. Clarifies accounting terminology a general businessperson would not be expected to understand
_____   5 Facilitates ease of reading and understanding through organization
_____   15 Facilitates ease of reading and understanding through standard spelling, grammar and structure

---

[a]Scofield and Combes, 1993, pp. 80-82.

Grading Criteria Sheet with Checklist

PROFESSIONAL REPORTING GRADE SHEET: PROFESSIONAL REPORT #3

Name: _____Grade: _____

CONTENT (75 points = 75%)
_____ 10 Cites appropriate SEC pronouncements
　　　　_____ ASR 268
_____ 10 Cites appropriate FASB pronouncements
　　　　_____ ARB 43
　　　　_____ SFAS 47
　　　　_____ ETTF 85-23
　　　　_____ ETTF 86-32
_____ 15 Classified balance sheets in accordance with GAAP and at least 1 in accordance
　　　　with SEC
　　　　_____ Note payable is short term
_____ 40 Provides comprehensive, insightful and logical support for balance sheet
　　　　recommended. Demonstrates an understanding of accounting policy choice.
　　　　_____ Understood SEC requirements
　　　　_____ Understood FASB requirements
　　　　_____ Private company
　　　　_____ Debt-to-equity ratio affected
　　　　_____ Net worth affected
　　　　_____ Characteristics of liability
　　　　_____ Characteristics of equity
　　　　_____ User needs
　　　　_____ Firm's self-interest
WRITING (25 points = 25%)
_____ 5 Writes in appropriate tone of controller to CEO. Clarifies accounting terminology
　　　　a general businessperson would not be expected to understand
_____ 5 Facilitates ease of reading and understanding through organization
　　　　_____ Introduction states accounting decision
　　　　_____ Conclusion summarizes accounting decision
_____ 15 Facilitates ease of reading and understanding through standard spelling, grammar
　　　　and structure
　　　　_____ A single firm is referenced by plural pronouns
　　　　_____ Homonyms are misused: there/their, its/it's
　　　　_____ Subject/verb disagreement

APPENDIX 4
HOLISTIC SCORING RUBRIC FOR CRITICAL THINKING[a]

FACIONE AND FACIONE

---

4   Consistently does all or almost all of the following:

Correctly interprets evidence, statements, and background information.
Identifies the salient arguments (reasons and claims) pro and con.
Thoughtfully analyzes and evaluates major alternative points of view.
Draws warranted, judicious, non-fallacious conclusions.
Justifies key results and procedures, explains assumptions and reasons.
Fair-mindedly follows where evidence and reasons lead.

---

3   Does most or many of the following:

Correctly interprets evidence, statements, and background information.
Identifies relevant arguments (reasons and claims) pro and con.
Offers analyses and evaluations of obvious alternative points of view.
Draws warranted, non-fallacious conclusions.
Justifies some results or procedures, explains reasons.
Fair-mindedly follows where evidence and reasons lead.

---

2   Does most or many of the following:

Misinterprets evidence, statements, and background information.
Fails to identify strong, relevant counter-arguments.
Ignores or superficially evaluates obvious alternative points of view.
Draws unwarranted or fallacious conclusions.
Justifies few results or procedures, seldom explains reasons.
Regardless of the evidence or reasons, maintains or defends views
    based on self-interest or preconceptions.

---

1   Consistently does all or almost all of the following:

Offers biased interpretations of evidence, statements, and background
    information, or the points of view of others.
Fails to identify or hastily dismisses strong, relevant counter-arguments.
Ignores or superficially evaluates obvious alternative points of view.
Argues using fallacious or irrelevant reasons, and unwarranted claims.
Does not justify results or procedures, nor explain reasons.
Regardless of the evidence or reasons, maintains or defends views
    based on self-interest or preconceptions.
Exhibits close-mindedness or hostility to reason.

---

[a]© 1994, Facione and Facione. The California Academic Press. Four level scale, version 1. Used by permission.

APPENDIX 5
SELF-ASSESSMENT MEASURE FOR PUBLIC SPEAKING

**Self-assessment Measure for Organization
in Public Speaking
Alverno College**[a]

a. Would an audience find a clear statement of direction and purpose near the beginning of my speech?
____ yes, for example _____
____ no
____ no, but I use a deliberate technique of suspense:_____

b. Did I, when necessary, relate the points I made throughout back to my main organizing idea?
____ yes, consistently, for example _____
____ occasionally, for example_____
____ no

c. Did I lead my audience from one part of my speech to the next with words and phrases that made the connection between individual parts clear?
____ yes, for example _____
____ occasionally, for example_____
____ no

d. Did I end with finality (i.e., clinch my argument, summarize or reassert, or propose some option or solution)?
____ yes, for example _____
____ no

Therefore I would rate my speech for ORGANIZATION:
(Circle number)

| Generally unclear organization | 1 | 2 | 3 | 4 | 5 | Generally clear organization |

---

[a]Loacker and others, 1984, p. 33.

APPENDIX 6
PEER RATING FORM - GROUP SKILLS,
LEADERSHIP AND CONFLICT RESOLUTION (BYU)[a]

COMPETENCIES: GROUP, LEADERSHIP, CONFLICT RESOLUTION

Section _____ Group No. _____ Date _____

Group Members (List alphabetically by name)
    #1_____   #2_____
    #3_____   #4_____
    #5_____

Observer's Name _____

2 = Meets expectations   3 = Exceeds expectations   1 = Below expectations

Student number	1	2	3	4	5
PREPARATION					
1. Comes to group prepared for task					
2. Completes assigned tasks on a timely basis					
PARTICIPATION					
1. Performs a meaningful role in the group					
2. Exhibits a positive disposition to a task					
3. Is willing to assume fair share of work					
INTERPERSONAL SKILLS					
1. Works compatibly with members of the group					
2. Shows good insight into how other members feel, think and act					
CONFLICT RESOLUTION					
1. Clearly identifies conflict situations					
2. Offers realistic and practical solutions					
3. Exhibits a desire to resolve conflicts					
LEADERSHIP					
1. Willingly assumes leadership role					
2. Clearly explains task when delegating					
3. Organizes task and clearly specifies goals					
4. Encourages others to participate in creative ways; does not hover over means					

You are encouraged to add comments below and on the reverse side.

_____

[a]BYU Core, 1992, Vol. II, p. 53.

APPENDIX 7
CHARACTERISTICS OF ORAL PRESENTATIONS[a]

I. Introduction
    A. Introduced content area
    B. Established mood and climate
    C. Motivated audience to listen and learn
    D. Conveyed usefulness of information or skill
    E. Established a knowledge base

II. Body
    A. Identified resources used
    B. Presented each point
    C. Paused to check understanding
    D. Directed attention to audience
    E. Maintained unobstructed view
    F. Reinforced important points
    G. Provided for review or audience feedback

III. Closure
    A. Introduced no new material
    B. Summarized major points
    C. Achieved objective
    D. Related to larger context

IV. Presentation Techniques
    A. Involved audience in the experience
    B. Provided reinforcement and feedback
    C. Used questioning techniques
    D. Exhibited interest and enthusiasm
    E. Used appropriate visual aids for emphasis

V. Verbal and Nonverbal Behaviors
    A. Voice
    B. Eye contact
    C. Gestures
    D. Movement
    E. Use of silence
    F. Facial expression

---

[a]Scofield, B. 1994 (November). Oral Communication Skills in the Accounting Classroom. Presentation at the 1994 Accounting Educator's Mini-conference, Portland, OR. Used by permission.

APPENDIX 8
LOCUS OF LEARNING MOTIVATION SCALE[a]

Select the letter which ranks the extent of your agreement with each statement, according to the following scale:

A   AGREE STRONGLY
B. AGREE
C. AGREE SLIGHTLY
D. DISAGREE SLIGHTLY
E. DISAGREE
F. DISAGREE STRONGLY

A number of questions may seem to be controversial, others you may feel neutral about; however, please attempt to choose the rating that best describes how you believe or feel.

1. There is a certain excitement in new learning of any kind, and it truly enriches life.
2. Learning that does not contribute to one's likelihood for occupational success is a waste of time.*
3. If you go to college for vocational purposes only, you miss a lot of other classroom learning experiences that are just as important if not more important.
4. General education and liberal arts have little appeal to me; I want to concentrate on the preparation necessary for vocational success.*
5. The search for meaning in life is given strong support by a mind that is continually looking for new learning, insights, and understanding.
6. If learning did not help me to get a better job and make a better living, I'd soon lose my motivation.*
7. A commitment to lifelong learning is a commitment to a rich and satisfying life.
8. The love of learning is what keeps me going.
9. The great values that university professors claim for liberal education are simply psychological justification for a way of life they have chosen and must defend.*
10. Learning is necessary in this world, but it is not something I find particularly enjoyable in itself.*
11. The evidence that people with more education earn more money is what really makes the case for higher education.*
12. The human being's desire to learn and understand is what makes the individual life worth living.
13. I am a person who is interested in a broad education rather than concentrating in one area.

---

[a]© 1992 Irvin Tom Nelson. Version 2.0. Items with an asterisk (*) are reverse scored. May be used for academic research with proper citation. Any use for commercial gain, without written consent, is prohibited.

APPENDIX 9
ACCOUNTING ATTITUDE SCALE[a]

Place a number next to each statement which ranks the extent of your agreement with each statement, according to the following scale:

1. AGREE STRONGLY
2. AGREE
3. AGREE SLIGHTLY
4. DISAGREE SLIGHTLY
5. DISAGREE
6. DISAGREE STRONGLY

A number of questions may seem to be controversial, others you may feel neutral about; however, please attempt to choose the rating that best describes how you believe or feel.

1. The CPA profession is well-respected.

2. Accounting is just a lot of rule-memorizing.

3. Accountants work alone more often than they work with people.

4. My peers would think I made a good career decision if I became an accountant.

5. Accounting is interesting.

6. Being an accountant has a lot of prestige.

7. Accounting is a lot of fixed rules; it doesn't involve conceptual skills or judgment.

8. Accounting is a profession, on a par with medicine and law.

9. Accountants find little personal satisfaction in their work.

10. I would enjoy being an accountant.

11. Accountants are boring people.

12. My family would like me to become an accountant.

13. I like accounting.

14. CPAs interact with many people.

---

[a]© 1991 Irvin Tom Nelson. Version 3.1. May be used for academic research with proper citation. Any use for commercial gain, without written consent, is prohibited.

APPENDIX 10
STAKEHOLDER SURVEYS: UNIVERSITY OF VIRGINIA

Assessment Survey of 4th Year Commerce Students

A. Demographics:

1. Age: _____ years

2. Sex: F   M

3. Race or Origin (circle only one):   **Foreign** (non-U.S. citizen),   **Hispanic,   African-American, Caucasian,   Native American,   Asian-American**

4. Virginia Resident: Yes   No

5. Transfer Student (entered McIntire from another University/School):   Yes   No

6. Please indicate your primary Concentration Area: **Accounting,   Finance,   Management,   MIS, Marketing**

7. Please indicate secondary Concentration(s) [circle as many as apply]:   **Accounting,   Finance, Management,   MIS,   Marketing,   Major/Minor outside of the Commerce School**

B. Satisfaction with McIntire Support Functions:

1. Were the requirements and procedures for admission clearly communicated prior to **Not clear** enrolling at the McIntire School of Commerce?   **at all**   **Perfectly clear**

                                 1   2   3   4   5   6   7

2. How could the Commerce School admissions policies and procedures be improved?

   _____
   _____

3. How would you rate the helpfulness of the Student Affairs Office (136 Monroe) on the following dimensions?

	Poor					**Excellent**	**Not applicable**
A. Registration	1	2	3	4	5	6	7	X
B. Drop/Add	1	2	3	4	5	6	7	X
C. Academic Requirements	1	2	3	4	5	6	7	X
D. Academic Problems	1	2	3	4	5	6	7	X
E. Personal Problems/Illness	1	2	3	4	5	6	7	X
F. Overall Effectiveness	1	2	3	4	5	6	7	X

4. How could the Student Affairs Office activities be improved?

   _____

5. How would you rate the Faculty on the following dimensions?

	Poor					**Excellent**	**Not observed**
A. Academic advice	1	2	3	4	5	6	7	X
B. Career advice	1	2	3	4	5	6	7	X
C. Advice on personal problems	1	2	3	4	5	6	7	X
D. Overall effectiveness of advice	1	2	3	4	5	6	7	X

6. How could the overall advising relationship between faculty and students be improved?

   _____
   _____
   _____

7. Please estimate how many times you met with faculty members outside the classroom during the Fall Semester.

   _____